Dark Psychology

3 Books in 1

Manipulation and Dark Psychology, How To Analyze People with
Psychology & Gaslighting. 41 Techniques to Defend
Yourself and Influence People With Dark Psychology Secrets

JASON ART

D1260734

The following Book is reproduced below with the goal of providing information that is as accurate and reliable as possible. Regardless, purchasing this Book can be seen as consent to the fact that both the publisher and the author of this book are in no way experts on the topics discussed within and that any recommendations or suggestions that are made herein are for entertainment purposes only. Professionals should be consulted as needed prior to undertaking any of the action endorsed herein.

This declaration is deemed fair and valid by both the American Bar Association and the Committee of Publishers Association and is legally binding throughout the United States.

Furthermore, the transmission, duplication, or reproduction of any of the following work including specific information will be considered an illegal act irrespective of if it is done electronically or in print. This extends to creating a secondary or tertiary copy of the work or a recorded copy and is only allowed with the express written consent from the Publisher. All additional right reserved.

The information in the following pages is broadly considered a truthful and accurate account of facts and as such, any inattention, use, or misuse of the information in question by the reader will render any resulting actions solely under their purview. There are no scenarios in which the publisher or the original author of this work can be in any fashion deemed liable for any hardship or damages that may befall them after undertaking information described herein.

Additionally, the information in the following pages is intended only for informational purposes and should thus be thought of as universal. As befitting its nature, it is presented without assurance regarding its prolonged validity or interim quality. Trademarks that are mentioned are done without written consent and can in no way be considered an endorsement from the trademark holder.

Table Of Contents

BOOK 2
HOW TO ANALYZE PEOPLE THROUGH PSYCHOLOGY

101

CHAPTER 2
THE CLUE TO REVEALING TRUE INTENTIONS – EYES 112

CHAPTER 3 POSTURE AND ORIENTATION 115

CHAPTER 4
NONVERBAL OF FEET AND LEGS 119

CHAPTER 5
NONVERBAL OF THE ARMS 122

CHAPTER 6
NONVERBAL OF THE HANDS AND FINGERS 125

CHAPTER 7
NONVERBAL OF THE FACE 130

BOOK 1

MANIPULATION AND DARK PSYCHOLOGY

A Practical Guide With More Than 31 Basic Strategies and Tips to Defend Yourself From Manipulators. Learn how Persuasion Techniques Work to Use Them to Your Advantage

JASON ART

Hello dear reader!

I hope you will enjoy this book.

I want to let you know how important your purchase and your judgment can be to me.

Just to give you a brief introduction: I'm a small writer, I write for passion and I think that the arguments of this book can help people to deepen into the topic, answer some questions and get the basis of your knowledge about the argument of this book. Writing a book is a great challenge that keeps you busy for hours on end, trying to create the best you can do.

Like the other independent writers, I don't have the giant advertising budget that many other publishers and businesses spend online.

So, one way that you can support my work is by leaving me a review on this book.

You can do it by using this QR code:

For an independent writer like me, getting reviews means I can submit my book for advertising.

So, every review means a lot to me.

I can't THANK YOU enough for this!

Enough with the words now, the book is waiting for you!

INTRODUCTION

Dark psychology is often defined as the study of a human condition relating to the psychological nature of humans to prey on others. Humans have the potential of victimizing others as well as living creatures. Although some people will exercise restraint, others act on their impulses. Thus, dark psychology tries to understand the perceptions, feelings, and thoughts that result in predatory human behavior.

In this book, we will look at several of the most commonly used techniques of the abusive personality types, and from there, we will spend time discussing how several of them can be used in a wider context, allowing for their usages during day-to-day interactions.

Unfortunately, for most people, you never really know that someone is preying on you until it's almost too late. Dark psychology makes an attempt at understanding the perceptions, feelings, thoughts as well as subjective processing systems that result in predatory behavior that is antithetical to the modern-day understanding of human behavior. It's assumed that 99.99% of the time, the motivation behind dark psychology is rational, purposive, and goal-oriented. This means that dark psychology is always present in the world as many people use tactics such as lying, persuasion, withholding love, and manipulation to get what they want. In most instances, these tactics are successful because they can read your mind. Thus, you can choose to either remain ignorant, live in denial and risk being a victim, or learn how you can protect yourself from psychological exploitation. When you understand the principles and ideas behind dark psychology, you will be better prepared to protect yourself from manipulation.

We will look into how these particular tactics impact the person that is being subjected to them. Some of these techniques work through instilling feelings in other people, knowing that emotions are incredibly motivating.

Common Dark Psychology Tactics

Dark psychology tactics may be overt or subtle. The most common tactics that most practitioners use are:

Reverse Psychology

When you employ this tactic, you will tell someone to do one thing, yet you know for sure that they'll do the opposite. It's this opposite action that a manipulator intended to happen.

Manipulative Vocabulary

When a manipulator uses this tactic, they will introduce into the conversation words that are common and have commonly accepted meanings to both parties, only for them to turn around later and tell you that they meant something else when using that word. The new meaning will in most cases change the definition making the conversation go in favor of the manipulator, even though you were tricked.

Restricting Choices

A manipulator who uses this tactic will limit your choices so that you get distracted from choices that you shouldn't pick.

Oversimplification

It's common for manipulators to oversimplify things, turning simple agreements into moral judgments and even casting themselves as angels. In such cases, you will hear them use phrases like "I'd never be able to forgive myself if I did what you did." Such statements will generally simplify a right or a wrong situation so that you're deemed to be unreasonable if you challenge their position. They don't accommodate or even acknowledge an alternate interpretation.

Withdrawal

Here, the manipulator will avoid you or give you silent treatment until you fulfill what they want from you.

Self-centeredness

Dark psychology manipulators tend to have a way of refocusing the center of an argument in their favor. It's common for them to say things like "I would never do that to you" while overlooking the complexity of the situation at hand. Some of the common words that show the tendency to overgeneralize include "always" and "never" that make it appear like a rule.

Love Denial

This is often difficult because the manipulator will make you feel abandoned or lost. It involves withholding love and affection until they get what they want from you.

Lying

This is surprising yet it's a common tactic among most manipulators. They will go to any length to lie about a situation. This could be through exaggerated or partial truth with the aim of getting you to act in a certain way.

Love Flooding

This usually involves complimenting, praising, or buttering up people in order for them to agree to your request. Love flooding often makes the victim feel good so that they're more likely to do something they'd otherwise have declined. You may also use this tactic to make someone feel they're attached to you, so that they do the things they'd normally not do.

Who Uses Dark Psychology?

Dark psychology is not only prevalent in romantic relationships. You will be surprised to know that it's also applicable within the public space as it can be used to get a desired response. Some of the people who commonly use these tactics include the following:

Sociopaths

One thing about sociopaths is that they're always charming, intelligent, and persuasive. What you don't know is that the motivation behind this is to get what they want. You will be surprised to know that they are often not emotional, and they don't feel any remorse. This explains why they are able to use dark psychology just to get what they want, even if it means forming superficial relationships.

Narcissists

Narcissists have a bloated idea of self-worth; hence, they thrive on making you believe they're superior. Such people will not shy away from using dark psychology and persuasion just to meet their desire to be adored and worshipped by everyone.

Politicians

Politicians employ dark psychology to convince the electorate to vote for them, not their opponent. They do this by making you believe that only their point of view is right.

Leaders

Just like politicians, many leaders have used dark psychology tactics to rally their subordinates, citizens, and even team members to do what they want.

Salespeople

Although not every salesperson will use dark psychology on you, most of them do. This is particularly true among salespeople who are very good at meeting and even surpassing targets because they don't even think twice before employing dark persuasion or manipulation.

Selfish people

People who are generally mean and like to put their needs first are more likely to use dark psychology to not have your needs concern them in any way. They're unwilling to forego their benefits; hence, they'd rather someone else lose, but not them.

CHAPTER 1
PRACTICAL AND HISTORICAL OVERVIEW

The foundations of the study of dark psychology are not modern. The models of classical comedy and tragedy during the height of the Greek Empire illustrate an understanding of this uniquely human capacity even during ancient times. The comedies and tragedies of ancient Greek theater were used as a means for society to experience catharsis—a collective exercise in which social bonding occurred by the creation and release of social tensions as a means of resolving societal conflicts.

But what is at the heart of this classical method of employing art as a means of regulating society is society's need to be regulated because of the unique capacity of human beings to act in ways that are destructive and harmful without any apparent practical purpose or necessity. This capacity is what clinical psychologists refer to as dark psychology.

Consider that species other than humans, such as lions, wolves, bears, or birds of prey, may track, target, hunt, and kill smaller, less powerful animals, such as deer, cattle, sheep, rabbits, and rodents. Yet, the reason for this predatory behavior is a necessity, not cruelty or malevolence. Also, when predatory animals hunt, they are likely to target the most vulnerable and the weakest, not out of any sense of meanness or malice, but because engaging with a weaker opponent involves less risk and less effort. Thus, the violence and destruction of natural predators serve practical needs—to feed themselves and their young to propagate their species.

Especially in the modern world, human beings have the advantage of education, positions of professional employment, the ability to grow and cultivate food, advanced language and communication systems, and a complex and interconnected system of world government, law, finance, and banking. As a result, there is no practical reason for any human being to engage in any act of predation or violence to secure the goals of food, shelter, and propagation. Because the system of laws punishes violence, such actions are detrimental to achieving these goals.

These habits and systems of living are unique to the human species, so it is reasonable to assume that they may require responses and abilities among the human members of society that are also unique. For example, lions and wolves are not capable of becoming doctors, plumbers, mechanics, or politicians, nor will they ever have any interest in doing so as these occupations are unique to the human species.

It is tempting to argue that human beings have developed their unique capacity for dark psychology as a means of propagating their survival in this unique environment. Take for instance a businessman who cheats on his taxes to gain an advantage in the business world, a lawyer who alters evidence to win a case, or a politician who lies to his constituents to win an election may be compared to the abilities of wild bears who hunt and killdeer or other game. Yet, animals in the wild never engage in predatory conduct that is marked by cruelty, maliciousness, or greed. Doing so would lead to their extinction.

We may understand that a business owner or banking professional would use every tool at his or her disposal to gain a competitive advantage. We may even understand the tendency among some professionals to work around laws rather than follow them when they see an economic advantage in doing so—when no real harm results, there is a practical goal that justifies the apparent abuse.

But often, criminal activity in human society does not have any practical justification. Within the unique sphere of human experience, dark psychology itself is a unique phenomenon. Defined broadly, it is the capacity for destructive and harmful behavior that serves no practical purpose whatsoever.

While all human beings have the capacity for dark psychology, many people do not act on these dark urges, choosing instead to channel that energy toward more productive and useful activities. Some people, however, do act on these dark urges to inflict gratuitous pain and harm on others.

Among those who are governed by dark psychology rather than by rational psychology, there is a continuum of deviant behavior ranging from mild forms of manipulation and dishonesty, usually motivated by some type of personal or financial gain; to acts of physical violence; and at the most end of the spectrum, the movement toward the "Dark Singularity," in which a person's psychology becomes so compromised by and addicted to deviant, aberrant, criminal, and malevolent misconduct that it becomes impossible for them ever to return to a rational mental state.

Historical tales of serial killers like Jack the Ripper remind us that this human failure is not new. Unfortunately, modern society appears to have embraced, at least to some limited degree, a complete rejection of all morality and social norms. The anonymity and access to power and information made possible by the invention of the internet has given these elements resources to establish for themselves a viable, permanent presence in human society. Understanding the nature and function of dark psychology has become an indispensable tool for anyone working to achieve success.

Before considering any further what "dark psychology" means, it may be more helpful to consider what "normal" means. Many historians and literary theorists have made the case that the evolution of human civilization has been accompanied by a steady erosion of social, moral, and cultural norms.

The word "more" (with the "e" pronounced as a long a, i.e., MOR-ay) is used to describe the social rules society enforces to encourage acceptable behavior. Many college graduates may remember taking a course from a sociology professor who required as a homework assignment that they deliberately identify and violate a more, then write a paper about the consequences. At one time, it was not uncommon for visitors to a college campus to enter an elevator and find themselves joined by a well-adjusted and successful college student who, for no apparent reason, faced the back of the elevator rather than the doors, thereby forcing uncomfortable and prolonged eye contact. This example of social deviance is very mild and can be viewed as even less threatening when we consider that it occurred in the context of a supervised experiment in the controlled and benign environment of a postsecondary educational institute.

Literature and humanities professors may help students examine this phenomenon in greater, and often more graphic and unforgettable, detail. For example, a pre-internet era literature course at a state university in California examined the transformation of cultural norms from 17th century France up through late 20th century America. In this course, the French novel, La Princesse de Clèves, was used to set a ground floor of social norms.

This novel portrays the life of a young woman living in the court of Henry II. Her mother had raised her with the greatest discipline to rise to the height of French society. As she enters adulthood, she is escorted to court to secure a prospect for marriage among the young noblemen. She eventually marries a young prince.

Already at this point in the novel, by today's standards, the main character of the novel would be considered successful beyond the reach of most people. However, her life does not proceed according to the ease and happiness we might expect. Instead, royal intrigue, gossip, and power struggles complicate matters. Although no actual wrongdoing ever really takes place, the young princess's hopes and ambitions are ultimately destroyed by the mere suspicion of infidelity. She is ultimately motivated by her sense of duty and obligation to enter a convent, where she dies in obscurity.

The course then uses literary works from intervening eras to trace the decline in the standards of human civilization from the virtuous heights depicted in La Princesse de Clèves through the dawn of the Industrial Revolution and ultimately to modern society at the end of 20th century America. The endpoint is illustrated by the violence, decadence, chaos, and alienation depicted in the late 20th century American novel, looking for Mr. Goodbar.

In this novel, a young school teacher, who, like the princess in the earlier novel, is an accomplished woman occupying an enviable position, is also seeking a prospect. However, her environment—the singles bars of New York City—is far removed from the royal court of 17th century France. Like the princess in the earlier novel, she too suffers a tragic fate at a young age when she is murdered by a young man she has met on one of her social outings.

Thus, defining social norms has become increasingly challenging, and many people have made the case that those norms are eroding as humanity progresses through its evolutionary cycles. We may refer to this tendency to develop destructive, negative, or harmful behavior as "dark psychology."

The emergence of "iPredators" as a class of offenders identified by clinical psychologists underscores the importance of understanding this area of psychology. New technology has expanded the power and speed through which dark psychology has found a way to manifest itself among many segments of human society; ICT has also magnified the degree to which such lifestyles have made themselves potentially viable, long-term means of living.

CHAPTER 2
PSYCHOLOGICAL MANIPULATION TECHNIQUES

Gaslighting

This is perhaps the cruelest form of manipulation. It is a means of casting into doubt the sanity and self-esteem of a person. You could say it is sowing the seeds of doubt into the victim of manipulation. Working on a similar principle such as "knowing you are being told repeated lies," until eventually you begin to believe the lies as the truth.

It is an unkind form of manipulation. The gas-lighter will cause their victim to lose all confidence in their own credibility. This completely destroys their self-worth as they begin to doubt themselves. That is the intention of gaslighting: to reduce the victim to a psychological mess. The manipulator will constantly put their target down by contradicting them and by convincing them that they are always wrong; sometimes to the point that the victim will be accused of telling lies. As a result of these, the victim loses all self-esteem.

When that happens, they become ruled by the domineering influencer. It is a form of mental abuse often seen in abusive personal relationships. The influencer will use constant techniques to make their victim doubt themselves.

Guilt and Sympathy

Guilt and sympathy can also be categorized as emotional blackmail. It's the most common technique used in personal relationships and plenty of time, it goes unnoticed. People are forced into doing things or favors for a partner as they bargain with your feelings for them. This is because it always works. This kind of manipulation can go on and on until the victim decides they have had enough. Emotional blackmail leads to partners having unhealthy relationships. During arguments, the partner uses threats or fear to have his or her way. Statements such as "if you leave me, I would rather commit suicide than let you be with someone else" are a norm in the relationship. Such words make you feel guilty about what will happen if you decide to go your own way.

Guilt tripping

A true form of emotional manipulation, a manipulator will exploit the integrity and conscientiousness of the victim by accusing them of being too selfish, too irresponsible, or not caring enough.

Shaming

Although shaming can be used to bring about social change when large corporations or governments advance abusive or discriminatory policies, manipulators may attempt to intimidate their victims by using sharp criticism, sarcastic comments, or insults to make them feel bad.

Blaming the victim

This tactic has become increasingly common. When a victim accuses a predator of abuse, the predator will attempt to turn it around by creating a scenario in which the victim alone is responsible for the harm that came to him. The predator may also try to accuse the victim of being the aggressor by complaining about the violation.

Seduction

This technique does not always have to involve sexual conquest or intimacy. Emotional predators may use flattery and charm to convince people to do their bidding, and they often look for people with low self-esteem.

Projection

This term is used in psychotherapy. Predators who use this technique will look for victims to use as scapegoats. When the manipulator does something wrong and is confronted, he or she will "project" his or guilt onto the victim in an effort to make the victim look like the responsible party.

Criticism

This is whereby the manipulator uses tactics such as belittling, dismissing, and ridiculing you. This keeps someone off-balance. Negative criticism is directed at a partner that makes them feel unworthy. The act of criticizing enables them to gain control over you. The manipulator creates a narrative that there is always something wrong with you and you are not good enough. This kind of narrative often makes you doubt yourself about what you feel and know. It can reach a point where you do not trust yourself.

Using Flattery, Kindness, and Charm

The use of kindness, charm, and flattery is often more damaging than is realized. The generous deployment of these techniques is a passive-aggressive type of behavior. The manipulator uses tactics such as gifting someone items, massaging their egos with flattery, and lots of compliments. One is left to question the real reason behind the compliments, expensive gifts, and paying lots of attention to the victim. These are acts done with ulterior motives, especially when they realize you are about to catch up on the manipulative state.

Lying

Lying is normally used by con artists. Manipulators lie practically about everything they see, hear, or know. They create a bunch of lies that are so complex that they tend to wrap people they cannot differentiate between reality and fake life. These lies can only be disputed by checking for inconsistency in the stories. When the deal is too good, think twice before accepting an offer. Abusers use this manipulation technique as they do not have fears about it. Lying can be caught if the victim decides to do a background check on the sources of information.

Caressing the Ego

Caressing the ego is most common in personal relationships. The manipulator caresses the ego of the victim by feeding them lies every time. The ego grows with time and in the end, the manipulator has you on their leash. This technique can be avoided if the victim of the act possesses humility.

Making Unusual Request before Your Real Request

This kind of manipulation technique is slightly mind-game oriented. The tactic involves asking an unusual request, mostly of a higher degree. This throws the person off-balance as he wasn't expecting such a request. The manipulator knew how that person was likely to respond, he would have asked for the usual request such as money, favor, shoes, etc. The victim was more likely to respond in the negative. This is because people's minds have been conditioned to avoid these tasks.

Voice-Raising and Irate Outbursts

Manipulators raise their voices during arguments to intimidate someone. They believed this process of raising the voice aggressively or loudly can enable them to achieve what they wanted. In a relationship, passion can come out in different forms such as tenderness, cute smiles you give one another, laughter, and the desire to share warmth in the arms of another. Passion, however, should not be mistaken by angry unpredictable outbursts during disagreements. In marriages or otherwise, couples tend to disagree with one another; this is not uncommon. However, there are various ways of handling conflict; having healthy communication with your partner is one such scenario; not screaming or having temper tantrums is another. The aggressive voice is sometimes accompanied by strong body language.

The manipulator can also start to pick quarrels on non-issues. When this starts to occur, it's a display telling you there are items needed to be ironed out. There are forces at play. In a relationship, someone who's picking random quarrels is either cheating on the partner or looking to end the relationship.

CHAPTER 3
UNDERSTANDING DARK TRIAD PERSONALITIES

Dark psychology is not a single, universally applicable medical diagnosis that can be applied across all cases of deviant personalities. There are, in fact, a wide variety of ways that dark psychology may manifest itself in someone's psychological and behavioral makeup. There is no absolute division of one deviant personality type from another, and many deviant personalities with prominent features of dark psychology may display elements of more than one manifestation of dark psychology.

It is important to remember that although the internet has spawned a huge growth in problems resulting from dark psychology, these traits have been part of human culture since ancient times. Another, narcissism, takes its name from an ancient mythological character.

Psychopathy

Psychopathy is defined as a mental disorder with several identifying characteristics that include antisocial behavior, amorality, and an inability to develop empathy or to establish meaningful personal relationships, extreme egocentricity, and recidivism, with repeated violations resulting from an apparent inability to learn from the consequences of earlier transgressions. Antisocial behavior, in turn, is defined as behavior based upon a goal of violating formal and/or informal rules of social conduct through criminal activity or through acts of personal, private protest, or opposition, all of which is directed against other individuals or society in general.

Egocentricity is a behavior where the offending person sees himself or herself as the central focus of the world, or at least of all dominant social and political activity. Empathy is the ability to view and understand events, thoughts, emotions, and beliefs from the perspective of others, and is considered one of the most important psychological components for establishing successful, ongoing relationships.

Amorality is entirely different from immorality. An immoral act is an act which violates established moral codes. A person who is immoral can be confronted with his or her actions with the expectation that he or she will recognize that his or her actions are offensive from a moral, if not a legal, standpoint. Amorality, on the other hand, represents a psychology that does not recognize that any moral codes exist, or if they do, that they have no value in determining whether or not to act in one way or another.

Thus, someone displaying psychopathy may commit horrendous acts that cause tremendous psychological and physical trauma and not ever understand that what he or she has done is wrong. Worse still, those who display signs of psychopathy usually worsen over time because they are unable to make the connection between the problems in their lives and in the lives of those in the world around them and their own harmful and destructive actions.

Machiavellianism

Strictly defined, Machiavellianism is the political philosophy of Niccolò Machiavelli, who lived from 1469 until 1527 in Italy. In contemporary society, Machiavellianism is a term used to describe the popular understanding of people who are perceived as displaying very high political or professional ambitions. In psychology, however, the Machiavellianism scale is used to measure the degree to which people with deviant personalities display manipulative behavior.

Machiavelli wrote The Prince, a political treatise in which he stated that sincerity, honesty, and other virtues were certainly admirable qualities, but that in politics, the capacity to engage in deceit, treachery, and other forms of criminal behavior were acceptable if there were no other means of achieving political aims to protect one's interests.

Popular misconceptions reduce this entire philosophy to the view that "the end justifies the means." To be fair, Machiavelli himself insisted that the more important part of this equation was ensuring that the end itself must first be justified. Furthermore, it is better to achieve such ends using means devoid of treachery whenever possible because there is less risk to the interests of the actor.

Thus, seeking the most effective means of achieving a political end may not necessarily lead to the most treacherous. In addition, not all political ends that have been justified as worth pursuing must be pursued. In many cases, the mere threat that a certain course of action may be pursued may be enough to achieve that end. In some cases, the treachery may be as mild as making a credible threat to take action that is not really even intended.

In contemporary society, many people overlook the fact that Machiavellianism is part of the "Dark Triad" of dark psychology and tacitly approve of the deviant behavior of political and business leaders who are able to amass great power or wealth. However, as a psychological disorder, Machiavellianism is entirely different from a chosen path to political power.

The person displaying Machiavellian personality traits does not consider whether his or her actions are the most effective means to achieving his or her goals, whether there are alternatives that do not involve deceit or treachery, or even whether the ultimate result of his or her actions is worth achieving. The Machiavellian personality is not evidence of a strategic or calculating mind attempting to achieve a worthwhile objective in a contentious environment. Instead, it is always on, whether the situation calls for a cold, calculating, and manipulative approach or not.

For example, we have all called in sick to work when we really just wanted a day off. But for most of us, such conduct is not how we behave normally, and after such acts of dishonesty, many of us feel guilty. Those who display a high degree of Machiavellianism would not just lie when they want a day off; they see lying and dishonesty as the only way to conduct themselves in all situations, regardless of whether doing so results in any benefit.

What's more, because of the degree of social acceptance and tacit approval granted to Machiavellian personalities who successfully attain political power, their presence in society does not receive the kind of negative attention accorded to the other two members of the Dark Triad—psychopathy and narcissism.

Narcissism

The term "narcissism" originates from an ancient Greek myth about Narcissus, a young man who saw his reflection in a pool of water and fell in love with the image of himself. In clinical psychology, narcissism as an illness was introduced by Sigmund Freud and has continually been included in official diagnostic manuals as a description of a specific type of psychiatric personality disorder.

In psychology, narcissism is defined as a condition characterized by an exaggerated sense of importance, an excessive need for attention, a lack of empathy, and, as a result, dysfunctional relationships. Commonly, narcissists may outwardly display an extremely high level of confidence, but this façade usually hides a very fragile ego and a high degree of sensitivity to criticism. There is often a large gulf between a narcissist's highly favorable view of himself or herself, the resulting expectation that others should extend to him or her favors and special treatment, and the disappointment when the results are quite negative or otherwise different. These problems can affect all areas of the narcissist's life, including personal relationships, professional relationships, and financial matters.

As part of the Dark Triad, those who exhibit traits resulting from Narcissistic Personality Disorder (NPD) may engage in relationships characterized by a lack of empathy. For example, a narcissist may demand constant comments, attention, and admiration from his or her partner, but will often appear unable or unwilling to reciprocate by displaying concern or responding to the concerns, thoughts, and feelings of his or her partner.

Narcissists also display a sense of entitlement and expect excessive reward and recognition, but usually without ever having accomplished or achieved anything that would justify such feelings. There is also a tendency toward excessive criticism of those around him or her, combined with heightened sensitivity when even the slightest amount of criticism is directed at him or her.

Thus, while narcissism in popular culture is often used as a pejorative term and an insult aimed at people like actors, models, and other celebrities who display high degrees of self-love and satisfaction, NPD is actually a psychological term that is quite distinct from merely having high self-esteem. The key to understanding this aspect of dark psychology is that the narcissist's image of himself or herself is often completely and entirely idealized, grandiose, and inflated and cannot be justified with any factual, meaningful accomplishments or capacities that may make such claims believable. As a result of this discord between expectation and reality, the demanding, manipulative, inconsiderate, self-centered, and arrogant behavior of the narcissist can cause problems not only for himself or herself, but for all of the people in his or her life.

The Dark Triad in Practice

The professional workplace has acknowledged the presence of people exhibiting Dark Triad characteristics. The following diagram illustrates that they are tolerated for their efficiency and their ability to get things done but contrasts that ability with the negative effects it has on their ability to form personal relationships:

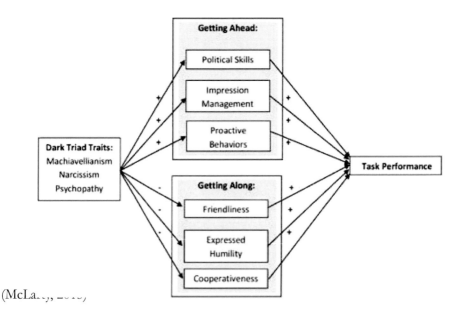

(McLa..., ...)

The remainder of this book discusses a wide variety of people and situations in which you may find one, two, all three, or some combination of these Dark Triad personalities working in concert around you.

The clinical descriptions are easy enough to categorize, and in isolation, it can be fairly straightforward to separate one type of dark psychology from another. However, the real world is a lot messier. Many of us have grown accustomed to so-called "toxic relationships," whether they are relationships with our partners, our co-workers, our family members, our bosses, or our political and community leaders. In addition, manifestations of dark psychology are often far more mundane than the dramatic examples we see in major television and film productions about the romantic lives of serial killers and other criminals. The more we accept these relationships as normal, the more difficult it will be to identify them as problematic.

Remember that psychological, emotional, and social predators do not think of themselves as sick. Their lack of morality and empathy, and their adaption from a very early age to live according to rules and methods you may find horribly wrong, can make their presence intimidating. However, you should also remember that even when their amorality and lack of empathy may allow them to enjoy an unjust advantage in relationships, their mental capacities are the result of underdevelopment, not a higher evolutionary state.

CHAPTER 4
WHAT IS EMOTIONAL MANIPULATION?

Covert emotional manipulation is used by people who want to gain power or control over you by deploying tactics that are both deceptive and underhanded. Such people want to change the way you think and behave without you ever realizing what it is they are doing. In other words, they use techniques that can alter your perceptions in such a way that you think that you are doing it out of your own free will. Covert emotional manipulation is "covert" because it works without you being consciously aware of that fact. People who are good at deploying such techniques can get you to do their bidding without your knowledge; they can hold you "psychologically captive."

When skilled manipulators set their sights on you, they can get you to grant them power over your emotional well-being and even your self-worth. They will put you under their spell without you even realizing it. They will win your trust, and you will start attaching value to what they think of you. Once you have let them into your life, they will then start chipping away at your very identity in a methodical way, and as time goes by you will lose your self-esteem and turn into whatever they want you to be.

Covert emotional manipulation is more common than you might think. Since it's subtle, people are rarely aware that it's happening to them, and in some cases, they may never even notice. Only keen outside observers may be able to tell when this form of manipulation is going on.

You might know someone who used to be fun and jovial, then she got into a relationship with someone else, and a few years down the line, she seems to have a completely different personality. If it's an old friend, you might not even recognize the person she has become. That is how powerful covert emotional manipulation can be. It can completely overhaul someone's personality without them even realizing it. The manipulator will chip away at you little by little, and you will accept minute changes that fly under the radar, until the old you are replaced by a different version of you, built to be subservient to the manipulator.

Covert emotional manipulation works like a slow-moving coup. It requires you to make small progressive concessions to the person that is trying to manipulate you. In other words, you let go of tiny aspects of your identity to accommodate the manipulative person, so it never registers in your mind that there is something bigger at play.

When the manipulative person pushes you to change in small ways, you will comply because you don't want to "sweat the small stuff." However, there is a domino effect that occurs as you start conceding to the manipulative person. You will be more comfortable making subsequent concessions, and your personality will be erased and replaced in a cumulative progression.

Covert emotional manipulation occurs to some extent in all social dynamics. Let's look at how it plays out in romantic relationships, in friendships, and at work.

Using Covert emotional manipulation

The ways in which a manipulator can act are innumerable, however they always follow basic strategies that generally have very precise mechanisms represented by the need to provoke feelings and emotions that all lead to the achievement of their goal.

Knowing these manipulative strategies allows you to create others that have the opposite task, that is to defend yourself from the manipulation itself.

The use of secret emotional manipulation is not particularly difficult as long as some specific steps are followed. The manipulator in fact lures its target by placing itself in a sort of role of reliability in the first place, for example by making friends with someone or placing itself in a position of relief and utility; secondly after he has made sure that he is in that position, he creates the ideal conditions to achieve his goal and makes the most of them, arousing the feelings we talked about before.

But what are these feelings then? And how does the manipulator provoke them?

Fear

This emotion is meant to guide you in defensive mode. When you trigger fear in someone else, you are trying to make them feel as if they should do something to ease that fear as quickly as possible. You can do this by trying to convince them that if they don't respect you, someone will get hurt or that there will be some other very negative result if they don't follow him. When you induce someone to respond to fear, you have already decreased their ability to think rationally, when people are afraid, their brains usually stop working properly. You trigger a response in which the blood that would normally function for greater cognition and rationalization is diverted to the body to prepare the muscles to fight or run away. The senses are sharpened, but the thinking skills are dampened. Usually, when you trigger fear, people will act in a way that will alleviate fear rather than rationally because they just want it to stop.

Sadness

When you activate sadness, you are unleashing a chain reaction of feeling hurt in some way. Usually, when someone feels sad, it is because they have experienced some sort of serious loss or significant defeat that is changing the perception of the world around them. Usually, these people just want to change the world around them to make them stop being how they perceive it and they will do anything to make it happen. This can be easily exploited: when you trigger sadness in someone else, you can then provide them with something you want them to do and make it appear as if that alleviates those feelings for them. In essence, you are convincing them to do something because you say it will ease that sadness, not because it will actually happen.

Fault

This is another of those negative emotions that with the aim of discouraging the repetition of a behavior that has led to a sort of failure. In this case, guilt is created when one cannot fulfill one of one's obligations. We all have obligations in life: these could be the obligations to pay our bills, to make sure that we get up in the morning to let the dog out to do their needs, go to work in order to earn a living, etc. Obligations drive us to ensure that needs are met and that everything is well taken care of. However, when we don't comply with these obligations, we tend to feel guilty.

Anger

Anger is used to make people react because it can be fomented and fed in many ways and it is not that difficult to do so. The difficult thing is to control it. When an angry reaction is triggered, you want to encourage someone else to feel like they need to go on the offensive. What happens is comparable to loading a spring that sooner or later will jump, bringing with so much energy that it will have to discharge itself in some way. Here the manipulator does just that, loads the spring of anger and then waits for it to explode and watch as it happens with all the consequences of the case. The consequences in this case lead to the goal of the manipulator. Anger is a difficult weapon to use. If the manipulator is not careful in managing and using this emotion and does not play his cards well, he runs the risk of turning against him

Emotional manipulator acts following this procedure:

It identifies its prey

it seeks with care and meticulousness the suitable person to satisfy its needs and that will make it reach its goal.

Lures his victim

After an emotional manipulator identifies his prey, he must lure it and first he does everything he can to get close to it and enter his life, appearing kind, empathetic, sensitive and altruistic. Obviously, he is lying in a very refined way so that the victim does not notice. Once the manipulator manages to invade your personal space and your private life, it will take very little time to show its true dark side, that is, selfish, arrogant and centralizing.

Builds feelings

Once he has gained the victim's confidence, he moves on to the next phase which consists in arousing one or more of the feelings described above. When you are able to make sure that you are able to create these emotions in the first place, you can begin this process. You have to be in a position where you can start triggering those feelings in the first place. This means that you have to make sure that you have some degree of relationship with the individual and therefore you need to be able to make sure you know how their minds work.

Exploits everything to his advantage

The manipulator finally exploits the consequences of the feelings provoked and the reactions that they entail all to his advantage in order to obtain his result and enjoy the fact of being able to achieve his goal.

Of course, there is more to emotional manipulation than just creating emotions in the first place. You also need to understand how you can take advantage of them. It is in the exploitation of emotions that you really start to see the changes you are looking for. It is when you are able to see those emotions emerge that you begin this process. You will take that emotion and connect it to what you want them to do. If you want them to doubt themselves, for example, you could trigger those feelings of guilt and then offer them other solutions.

Indicators of emotional manipulation

Speaking of emotional manipulation, it is clear that for 90% of cases we are talking about a manipulation that takes place within a couple relationship or between two individuals between whom there is a relationship and a very close bond therefore, as soon as the actual manipulation, the victim or those around them will notice one or more of the following signs:

- Recurring nightmares

- Frequent feeling of bewilderment or confusion

- Little confidence in one's sense of reality

- Inability to remember the details of discussions with the manipulator

- Symptoms of anxiety: gastric disorders, tachycardia, chest tightness, panic attacks

- Fear or agitation in the presence of the manipulator

- Effort in telling yourself and friends that the relationship with the manipulator is fine

- Discussions with friends and relatives about your relationship with the manipulator

- You can no longer feel joy and satisfaction in your life - Sadness, until depression

- Anger

Characteristics of a Manipulative Relationship

First, one theory states that emotional manipulation is essentially a one-sided activity in which all of the effort to create, execute, and sustain a manipulative relationship is made by the manipulator. Such relationships generally have three defining characteristics:

1.Concealment: The true motivations of the manipulator—aggression and control—are concealed by behavior that appears friendly and helpful.

It is more difficult to conceal problems with aggression and control in our personal, intimate relationships, our friendships, and our relationships among family members. As a result, these types of relationships are more likely to develop in the workplace or in your community among business owners and their staff or other professionals.

For example, you may encounter a co-worker who, on the surface, is always friendly toward you at work. This person may always be willing to find a place for you at the table during lunch break or may always appear at your cubicle with a smile and offer lots of encouragement and advice. This type of conduct by itself may be a good sign. However, if this relationship ultimately leads to a friendship outside of the office, an emotional manipulator may misinterpret your intent.

In the less-regulated world outside of the workplace, emotional predators may exploit the trust they have established by making unreasonable demands on your time, asking for favors, and putting pressure on you to agree by suggesting there could be repercussions at work. A truly gifted manipulator will know how to make this threatening behavior look and feel friendly and perfectly reasonable until you have been too badly compromised to take any action to reverse course.

2.Profiling: The manipulator will have studied the vulnerabilities of the victim, so that he or she will be able to exploit them more effectively.

This type of predatory conduct has become much worse in the current environment of surveillance and social networking sites.

Often in the work environment, this type of personality can manifest itself without your awareness. Especially if you work for a large company, anyone who has access to personnel records or other sources of information may feel they have the luxury to profile you so that when they do finally approach, they will appear quite calm and confident.

If someone with whom you have had little or no direct contact seems to know a lot about you, you should be cautious. Often, being overly enthusiastic, paying you a lot of compliments, and telling you that you have earned a great reputation is a technique used to hide the true intentions of the manipulator.

3.Amorality: The manipulator will possess high degrees of amorality and a lack of remorse, both of which enable behavior that is ruthless, cunning, and treacherous.

Often, we expect that a simple, polite request to cease harmful, rude, or disruptive behavior should be sufficient to end predatory or violative misconduct. Although we may be right, Dark Triad personalities who lack empathy find it easy to engage in amoral behavior. Even worse, far from feeling any remorse as a result of committing abuses, they often feel a great sense of joy, victory, and accomplishment. As the saying goes, such reactions add insult to injury.

Further, in the competitive business environment, this type of dishonest and illegal behavior may be rewarded. Meanwhile, the efforts of diligent, honest employees may go unrewarded, and their complaints of abuse may result in punishments levied against them rather than the perpetrators.

Categories of Emotionally Manipulative Behavior

Understanding the basic dynamics of manipulative and abusive relationships is important. Each of these general types of relationships may be characterized by specific types of behavior. Psychologists have identified many specific techniques of behavior modification commonly employed by emotional manipulators. Some of these techniques include:

- **Positive reinforcement:** This technique was identified by the behavioral psychologist B.F. Skinner, whose theory of operant conditioning resulted from his experiments with small animals placed in cages. In his experiment to prove the theory of positive reinforcement, he used cages equipped with two levers—one lever did nothing, while the other produced a food pellet whenever the small animal pushed it. Soon, the animals learned through positive reinforcement which lever to push to get their reward.

Emotional manipulators employ positive reinforcement in their strategies by using techniques such as praise, false and superficial demonstrations of emotions such as charm and sympathy, excessive rewards including gifts, money, approval, and attention, and other outward demonstrations of emotion meant to make the victim feel good.

- **Negative reinforcement:** The other part of Skinner's experiment proved the effectiveness of negative reinforcement. For this part of his experiment, small animals were again placed in cages, which were again equipped with two levers. This time, the cages were charged with a mild voltage of electricity that caused slight discomfort to the animals that were placed in them. Once inside the cages, the animals would press one of the two levers. One of the levers did not produce any results, while the other stopped the electrical current, relieving the discomfort. Soon, the animals learned to press the lever that lessened their pain.

- **Intermittent reinforcement:** Intermittent reinforcement can be either positive or negative and is used to create doubt, fear, or uncertainty. An emotional manipulator may "train" his or her victim by imposing inconsistent reward and punishment mechanisms to lessen the victim's sense of confidence, control, and autonomy.

For example, in a romantic relationship, the predator may condition the victim to wear certain clothing, listen to certain music, eat certain types of food, and work at a certain type of job. As the victim in this relationship gains confidence, the predator may begin to discourage their victim, who will be caught off guard. As the victim scrambles to respond, the manipulator may again change tactics.

• **Punishment:** Punishment is a very basic form of emotional manipulation that may involve an entire range of psychologically and emotionally negative and damaging behavior, such as threats, yelling, nagging, complaining, intimidation, insults, guilt, and other forms of emotional blackmail. Skilled predators may find a way to incorporate this abusive and controlling behavior into the relationship over time, so that the victim will develop a tolerance for abuse.

• **Traumatic one-trial learning:** This technique is related to the use of punishments, but rather than a feature of a long-term relationship, these techniques involve discrete episodes in which the manipulator uses verbal abuse, demonstrations of anger, and other forms of dominance and intimidation to discourage the victim from certain types of behavior.

CHAPTER 5
SIGNS THAT YOU'RE BEING MANIPULATED

The type of people that the manipulative people target is low self-esteem people, no boundaries people, and desperate people. Now how do you know if you are being manipulated? If you feel like you are constantly criticized and he makes you feel inadequate, then it means you are being manipulated. If you get into an argument and he's giving you the silent treatment, you are being manipulated. If somebody gives you the silent treatment, which makes you go crazy, you start thinking of every scenario, and you start making assumptions because no dialogue is happening that can reassure or bring clarity to your thoughts, then that is a huge form of manipulation.

You sense fear, duty, and guilt

Coercive conduct comprises three factors: anxiety, responsibility, and guilt. "When someone manipulates you, you're mentally coerced to do something that you usually don't really want to do. You could feel afraid to do so, compelled to do so, or guilty of not doing so.

I refer to two different manipulators: "the abuser" and "the victim." an abuser makes you feel afraid and will use violence, threats, and coercion to manipulate you. The victim instills a sense of guilt in their target. "Usually, the victim acts hurt. But although manipulators frequently play the victim, the fact is they're the ones who created the problem.

An individual approached by manipulators who acts as the victim always attempts to support the manipulator to avoid feeling bad. Targets of this type of manipulation frequently feel responsible for assisting the victim to stop their suffering by doing everything they can.

Strings are connected

If you don't get a favor just because, then it's not 'for fun and free. "If strings are applied then there is trickery.

One manipulator form is "Mr. Nice man.' This person will be supportive and offer other people plenty of favors. "It's really complicated, but you don't know anything that's bad. "But, on the other side, there is a rope connected for any positive deed — an obligation." If you don't fulfill the standards of the manipulator, you'll be forced to feel ungrateful. In fact, one of the most common forms of trickery is to exploit the rules and standards of reciprocity.

For example, a salesman could make it appear like you would purchase the product since he or she offered you a discount. A spouse in a partnership can buy you flowers and then ask for something in return. "These techniques operate as it violates societal expectations. "It's normal to return the favor but we often still feel it necessary to reciprocate and comply even if someone does one insincerely.

You recognize the methods of 'foot-in-the-door' and "door-in-the-face

Manipulators frequently try out one of two strategies. The first one is the strategy of foot-in-the-door, in which somebody starts with a simple yet rational request — like, do you have a moment? — Which then contributes to a bigger request — like I want 10 dollars for a taxi. That's commonly used in street frauds.

The door-in-the-face method is the opposite — it includes somebody making a large request, having it rejected, and then asking a smaller favor.

For e.g., anyone doing contract work can ask you for a large amount of money upfront, and afterward, ask for a lesser proportion after you've refused. This works since, according to me, the smaller appeal appears comparatively rational after the larger demand.

You interrogate yourself

Frequently, the term "gaslighting" is used to recognize manipulation that causes people to question themselves, their actuality, consciousness, or thoughts. A dishonest individual can distort what you're saying to make it about them, hijack the discussion or make you sound like you've done something bad when you're not entirely sure you've done it.

If you're being emotionally manipulated, you may experience a false sense of shame or defensiveness — like you utterly lost or had to do something wrong when, in fact, that's not the case.

Ghosting You

And guys do this a lot, even if it is something as simple as ghosting you. Because it trains you to not get used to hearing from him certain times, and you always have to reach out to see how he is doing and checking out to see if he remembers the date that he set for you. They use their profession or their education to delay you finding out the truth or make you feel like they're always the right one. For instance, if you get into an argument with someone and you are dating a lawyer, they will tell you something like, "I've been a lawyer for five years, and I know what I'm talking about and people that did what you just did need not to be trusted." They sort of use their title to rain over you and make it look like they are the right ones. What happens is that you silently agree to what they are saying because they do know what they are talking about. Because they know when people lie, and they know it through body language. Demonize your reactions

They tend to demonize your reactions because anytime someone that is manipulating you and they don't want you to be able to express yourself or control the situation, they're going to make you feel like you are the bad guy for reacting the way that you did to the situation. They will flip the script on you because you didn't agree with their actions.

You might tell him, "Hey, babe, I don't know why you just liked this girl's picture on Instagram. I thought that we agreed that you are not going to do this. You show me their stuff. Because it makes me feel embarrassed that my boy is licking the girl's photos and commenting on rubbish on Instagram, and it makes me feel insecure because you are my boyfriend". Then he will say something like, "you are so insecure it's just Instagram, I can't believe that you are seriously talking to me about a comment that I wrote to a girl. First of all, I don't even know her, and she looks nice. Other guys are commenting on her photos, but why do you care because I'm with you". So, they demonize you and make you feel like the way you feel is not accounted for. They make you feel like the way you feel is invalidated because he doesn't know that girl, and maybe he may even be trying to learn that girl.

Using pity

One of the greatest forms of manipulation is by using pity. Because getting pity out of anybody is going to guilt-trip them, so that they feel bad for you and do what you say and hear you out and like whatever trash you want to slip by because they are feeling bad for you.

For instance, if you say, "I just realized that when we were in the get-together, you were nagging to really hang out with me. You were just doing your own thing. I don't know everybody there, I felt alone, and I understand that you know everybody, but I didn't feel included. Then he will say something like, "Honey, I'm really sorry that you didn't feel included. However, what do you expect me to do, all the people were people that I grew up with. So, I'm sorry that I wasn't holding your hand the entire time. But I did introduce you to some people. You know that I wouldn't do that to you. You know that I am not like that. I was just caught up. Plus, I saw one of my girls from high school and we just started talking. Come on, if you really know me, you know that I wouldn't do something like that. I am not like that."

So, they tried to play on your emotions so that you will think that they are helping you. To think something like, oh, "I do know him. I'm not sure that anyone will want to invite me somewhere and then drop me off and not even associate with me at all or leave me alone". So, you feel bad for yelling at him because it gets overwhelming when you are hanging out with so many people that you haven't seen in a long time.

If you are bothered by the fact that he left you alone, then it means that he left you alone for so long that it became so uncomfortable. It's not a big deal if he's going to leave you for some minutes and go to say hi to someone, but he should introduce you to those people because you guys are in a relationship. So, the reason why you are feeling how you are feeling is because something was wrong.

So, the best way to combine this is to minimize their actions so that you get to stick around. If he says, "I can't believe you would do something like that. You should say, "what do you mean. You do dumb things all the time". These people that always want to downplay what it is that they are doing so that you will feel stupid and feel like you're overreacting on what the offense was.

For instance, let's say that you want to surprise him and leave something cute in his mailbox. So, you drive by his house, and you see another car parked in his driveway, and then you notice that another girl is in his house. And then you think that maybe that is one of his guy friend cars so you drive in his car and instead of giving him a little bit of a surprise, you get out of the car because you don't know whose car you are seeing. You knock on the door and then he opens the door halfway and starts asking you what things like, "What are you doing here." And then you answer him, "I'm checking in. Are you well? I noticed that there is an extra car in the driveway, and it's not mine. So why are you not letting me in". and he says, "that is one of my homegirls from high school we haven't talked in a long time, and she just wanted to drop by and catch up."

So, you should say, "why is your friend in your house alone and you didn't even mention it to me. I've never seen this girl in my life, and I never knew that this is one of your homegirls. Why am I just finding out about this"? And he says, "calm down you're just a little extra obnoxious, she's just a friend. She just dropped by to say hi. I didn't even think about mentioning it to you, because it's not about what you think. Because if it was like that, you would just tell me," then he's trying to ignore and because he wants you to feel guilty. He wants you to feel like how can he cheat on you in broad daylight when he knows that you can come and visit his house. The best way that this guy used to hide things in plain sight is because it's so unbelievable.

Glaring and Unbelievable things

They do glaring and unbelievable things, then they try to convince you that what you saw wasn't true. And what you saw couldn't be what you possibly think. It is because it doesn't look like you will do anything like that, and he will have to be a real idiot to do something like that to you. He wants to minimize his action and play ignorant like he has no idea what it is, and you are tripping, and both of them are just friends. He also tries to make rude remarks in the name of humor.

It's so important that it's it in your subconscious mind, and whenever you guys are in an argument or in a situation where you feel intimidated, and you're someone that is easily intimidated by other beautiful girls, then what he says becomes your inner voice. So, the joke that he makes about how big your nose gets into your mind. Because you are thinking about the waitress and it's looking like he's flirting with her because she has a nose that he actually likes or he always makes fun of your crooked tooth, and you are very subconscious about that, and the girl over there has straight teeth.

So, you must pay attention to things like that in the relationship and in friendships because there is always some sort of truth to those little remarks. There is always some sort of underlying truth if somebody is constantly attacking something about you like your physical appearance or playing on your weaknesses because they know that it is going to get you inevitably. But, remove any responsibility or accountability for what they are saying even though they're trying to make it look like a joke.

Signs That You Are Exploited in a Relationship

Manipulation was a massive topic of consideration when I worked with couples. It's a normal tactic that offenders and controlling spouses use as it's impossible to show, it lets the person who is being used seem like it's his own mistake, and it's easier to deal with it. Most people are not even aware that they are being exploited until it is very late. Hence, the issue of trust rises.

Though you do not notice it all the time, there are certain indications that your spouse is holding your mind. It might help to educate yourself so as to accurately identify when you are being manipulated if you detect those indications. And hopefully, motivate you to get to know a partner that doesn't have to use crooked tactics to control you in order to feel safe regarding your relationship.

Simple Ancient Bullying

It is among the less complex (and more readily identifiable) ways of coercion. Say, your partner asks you, for example, if you'd like to clean the car they use. You don't and you just want to tell them "no". However, the manipulative look on their forehead and their manner of speech tells you to clean their car, or else bad things can happen. So, you end up saying "I would like to", and you end up doing it. The type of person who uses the violence threat to handle you and convince you to do things you wouldn't like to do might later claim something like, "You really didn't have to be doing that. You must have denied that." This will make them seem like the nice person, and it's your mistake because you did not get your task finished.

Blackmailing Emotionally

Blackmailing someone emotionally is disgusting because it does not contribute towards a healthy and stable relationship. It feels like, "I'm going to destroy everything including myself if you quit." Or, it might even look like, "I'm not going to live without having you in my life." It may be emotional or subtle. It's essentially a strategy that utilizes terror, remorse, and humiliation to hold you under the control of your partner. Decide if you want to stay in a relation just because someone told you that he/she will commit suicide if you did not comply. You are not solely responsible for the complete wellbeing of another person.

Solution: Don't fall prey to it. It's always a sign of manipulation and it is not a serious sign of self-harm or suicide. But in order to be in a safe place, say, "If you are feeling depressed, I'm calling the ambulance or cop for the sake of help, but I will not be the one to work with it." It may sound cruel, but it's really the only thing you could do.

Playing victim card

Let's portray an example for you. Your companion and you start to fight. Irrespective of who's wrong, what's been said or what's really happened, your partner's so sad and cannot imagine you'd damage their heart like that. Even though your partner's probably the one who's done bad things, and without considering how you've responded, you are the one who is always apologizing, and your companion almost always is needy of extra attention and love. This way you consider yourself an irresponsible, rude partner and your companion gets away with their actions.

Apologize only for the things you should be apologetic for. Do not give up on the relentless efforts of your wife to pressure you into slipping on your knife. Tell something like, "I'm so sorry that I was angry and increased my voice. It was unnecessary. But I will not apologize for getting mad with what you've done. Here's how it made me think and feel.

Convenient Neediness

If things do not go the way your companion wants, are they weak or ill, or require treatment and support? In reality, this is a form of manipulation, even when your companion is very ill. Few examples: your spouse does not really want to go through tough discussion with you because they feel anxious. Your partner does not feel like going someplace and immediately you won't be able to go either since they were looking for you to get help in overcoming their anxiety. Your companion is unwilling to assist you with house work since they are suffering from a fever or lack the strength. Your partner does not want to be left alone, because who is going to be worried about them? Or might be possible they have medical issues so you will feel bad for your partner and pay extra attention to them.

Where to go: That is a sign of a not-so-successful relationship, and you're probably going to need to think about that. But for now, you should determine how you can care for your companion when you go and do what you have to do. Chances are, they're going to be okay.

Gaslighting

Gaslighting is the most likely form of manipulation to make you feel like you're losing your mind. Your spouse is doing questionable stuff regularly, including pretending they didn't say something, pretending you didn't say anything, leaving out facts, manipulating the truth, reinventing the history, making you remember things you've overlooked, and having you feel like you're failing them in general.

CHAPTER 6
SPECIFIC EXAMPLES OF EMOTIONAL MANIPU-LATION

Insisting on meeting at certain locations: Manipulators may try to get the upper hand by insisting on a so-called "home court advantage," thereby forcing you to function in a less familiar and less comfortable environment that diminishes your personal negotiating power.

Examples:

If you have a dispute with a professional acquaintance or colleague, they may insist on always meeting in their office or at a café or restaurant that is more difficult for you to travel to.

If you are in a personal relationship, your partner may always insist that you meet him or her at their favorite spot and meet with their friends. They may show little interest in reciprocating when you invite them to participate in social activity you find rewarding.

Premature intimacy or closeness: The manipulator will immediately shower you with affection and reveal all sorts of intimate secrets.

Examples:

In a personal relationship, the manipulator may introduce themselves using phrases like, "No one has ever made me feel like this before. I know we were made for each other."

This type of intimacy and closeness can happen in the professional environment, too. A colleague you don't know very well may make comments like, "You know, I have been watching you work, and I can see how skilled and talented you are. No one else really gives you the credit you deserve."

Managing conversations by always requiring you to speak first: In professional relationships, this is commonly used as a sales and negotiation technique to mine you for your information to make a more lucrative sale.

Examples:

A salesperson may say something like, "Rather than bore you with details about our products or services, why don't you tell me about yourself and how you think we can help you?"

In personal relationships, this technique can be used to gain a power advantage. Skilled manipulators will conceal their true motives by saying things like, "I may have been wrong, but first I'd like to hear your side of the story."

Distorting or twisting facts: Whether in personal or professional relationships, manipulators will use conversational techniques to distort facts in an effort to make you doubt yourself and back down.

Example:

A manipulator may use a phrase like, "I understand how you feel. I'd be angry, too. But the truth is, I never made that comment. I don't think your memory of that conversation is accurate. I know what you really meant to say was that…"

Intellectual bullying: An emotional manipulator may use an unnecessarily large volume of statistics, jargon, or other types of factual evidence to impose a sense of expertise.

Example:

Someone who is implementing the tactic of intellectual bullying may say something like, "This is not an easy decision to make. In addition to all the legal and financial considerations, you also have to consider how this will affect people at work and the rest of the family. I know technology is not your strong point, but I have already done all the heavy lifting in that regard. Now, we only have a limited amount of time, and I know how important this is for you. I wish we could just take our time and think about it. Fortunately, I have already evaluated all the major concerns, and I can make it really easy for you to make a decision."

Bureaucratic bullying: This technique is similar to intellectual bullying. Unfortunately, this technique may indicate that someone is abusing their position of authority by insisting on placing as many obstacles, red tape, or other impediments in the way of what should be a straightforward resolution.

Example:

Such a person may make a statement such as, "I understand your concerns, but I would encourage you not to pursue this any further. You have a legitimate complaint, but the expenses and time required will likely cost more than you will get in return. Also, if you make any missteps, you may have to spend the next several years filling out paperwork and going to court hearings."

Examples:

A manipulator may try to make you feel bad for voicing your concerns by saying something along the lines of, "I understand that you are voicing an important objection, but have ever stopped to consider what will happen to the rest of the team if you eventually get your way?"

Manipulators may also try to discourage you by making light of your problems. For instance, "I know how bad you feel right now, but before you do anything, make sure you keep it in perspective. You know, this time last year I was facing a crisis ten times worse, and all I did was sit it out."

Insults and put-downs: Manipulators are good at following up rude or mean-spirited comments with sarcasm or some other attempt at humor to make it seem like they were joking.

Example:

"I know you really worked hard on that presentation. It's too bad you wasted your time, though. But, hey, no worries. I'm sure it will be great preparation when you interview for your next position."

Refusing to take responsibility: There are a variety of ways a skilled manipulator can accomplish this goal by using evasion, denial, or feigning ignorance or confusion.

Examples:

"You didn't tell me I had to finish the project by today."

"I know that's not what you wanted, but everyone else agreed that it should be fine this way."

"What do you mean by accountability? I don't remember discussing any of that with you."

"Can you explain the problem with this project again? It's really too hard for most people to understand."

Competitive responses: Manipulators may introduce outside, unrelated issues to convince you that your concerns are less important.

Example:

"I do understand you've been placed in a difficult situation, but you should think about me. Right now, you have already passed all the sales goals I wanted to achieve for this year. It's bad enough that you're making me look bad. Now you're forcing me to ignore my own workload just so I can help you out."

Excessive criticism: Hypercritical people often have problems with low self-esteem. They will use this technique to make them feel better about themselves. Often these efforts can be very blatant, obvious, and hurtful.

Examples:

"You shouldn't wear that. It makes you look fat and ugly."

"You shouldn't talk so much in meetings. You usually just end sounding stupid."

Projecting blame: Manipulators can place you in a position in which you are forced to take responsibility for their actions.

Example:

"I know that meeting didn't go the way you had hoped. I tried to tell you not to pick me to lead the meeting. Next time, you should listen to me."

Using guilt and ultimatums: Manipulators do not have to resort to physical violence. Often, delivering an ultimatum while making you feel bad can force you to act in ways you otherwise wouldn't.

Example:

"Remember what happened last year when I asked you to decide where to go for the Christmas holiday? The entire holiday was ruined because you took too long to decide, and then you made everyone stay home instead of taking the trip back home. This year is going to be different. If you don't decide by the end of the day, we're never going to invite you to another Christmas party again."

Indirect communication: This has become an increasingly common technique used by manipulators and bullies and often involves the use of gossip and rumors.

Example:

"You can forget about the funding for that project we had planned. I know you told me to wait until the meeting tomorrow, but I already talked to the boss and told him it was a bad idea."

The silent treatment: In the connected world of digital communication, many manipulative people will simply ignore text messages, email messages, and voicemails as a way of letting you know they do not approve of something you have done.

Gaslighting: The manipulator will make blanket statements to draw your credibility and judgment into question. Manipulators are highly adept at lying, then imposing the falsehood on you until you accept it and back down.

Examples:

Suppose you are at work, and you have documented a pattern of workplace violations that are costing you time and money. The manipulator may try to gaslight you by first requesting to see the evidence with a sincere expression of concern.

"I see. You definitely have a very convincing case. Let me see if I can find out what's going on so we can get to the bottom of it."

Subsequently, using a combination of denial, indirect communication, and feigned ignorance or confusion, the manipulator may return to you in a couple of weeks with a different response.

"I know I agreed with you at first. But I was talking to the other guys. I think you might have a couple of the dates wrong. Also, I know it seems like a big deal, but most of the other guys were saying they do this kind of thing all the time, and it's never a problem. Wait, what was the law or rule or whatever you were talking about again? It seemed really important when you were talking about it, but no one else seemed to know anything about it. I don't know… Maybe you're just overreacting."

Using negative surprises: Many people in both personal and professional relationships will use "negative surprises" to maintain power in a relationship and manipulate and control people.

Example:

In the workplace, you may have been encouraged by members of management to follow a specified path that will lead to a promotion and a raise. After you have put in overtime and gone above and beyond to meet all the demands, the boss makes an announcement at the meeting where you expect to be promoted:

"I know James has been working very hard these past few months, and we all appreciate his inspirational efforts to increase our sales numbers. I am also glad you are all here to hear who will be promoted to the position of District Manager. We just got word this morning that I will be personally assuming the new role, while also maintaining my current position."

Playing the martyr: Manipulators use this technique to establish control.

Examples:

A manipulator's initial reaction when you ask them to help with a special project might be:

"Sure! Great! Let me know how I can help!"

However, once the assignment or project is underway, their comments will be entirely different.

"I know I said I was eager to help, but this is really too much. This workload is such a burden. I wish I had never agreed."

"Of course, I agree. Really, it's not a problem. You're just being overly sensitive and paranoid. You shouldn't worry so much."

The goal here is to make you look like the bad guy, call your credibility into question, and undermine your authority.

CHAPTER 7
FACTORS THAT MAKE YOU VULNERABLE TO MANIPULATION

The other side of avoiding the trap of toxic relationships with emotionally manipulative people is to consider whether you have any of the personality traits predators look for in those they are most likely to victimize.

Many of us expect to be treated with respect and kindness and according to the basic laws and customs of educated, civilized, responsible adulthood. We take this understanding for granted and expect for it to be a given in all of our relationships. We consider this to be the default understanding in our relationships not only among those we know and trust, but perhaps even more so among strangers, co-workers, and professionals with whom we may come into contact. Unfortunately, emotional predators are well aware of this expectation and often exploit this area of trust specifically when looking for ways to exploit victims.

We have all seen films about the nice-looking stranger who asked for help with a flat tire or the new neighbors who seemed so nice when they first moved in. Slowly, these relationships that seem so benign and normal on the surface quickly spiral into a seemingly inescapable nightmare of violence, victimization, and criminality. Though we are right to regard these types of relationships as the exception rather than the rule, they have unfortunately become more common. As a result, becoming more self-aware is an equally important aspect of avoiding manipulation and exploitation as looking for signs of abuse in those around you.

The following list covers many of the characteristics that emotional manipulators consider weaknesses and will try to exploit. If you believe you may display any of these characteristics, remember that it does not mean you are a weak person or deficient, nor does it mean that you deserve to be exploited or manipulated. However, you should remember that, right or wrong, if you are too open about these types of behaviors, you may be placing yourself directly in the path of an emotional manipulator who is looking for a new victim.

Over-eagerness to please other people:

Often a competitive work environment or even the natural environment of your personal relationships rewards achievement. Normally, that's a good thing. But take care to monitor for changes in the environment. People who naturally work to achieve success can be taken advantage of by being placed in a disadvantageous position.

Addiction to earning approval and recognition:

This trait is different from the trait of the narcissist, who feels entitled to excessive approval and recognition, even without having done anything to earn it. Yet, demonstrating an addiction to recognition and approval may signal to anyone with high degrees of dark psychology that you are an easy target.

Fear of expressing negative emotions:

Often manipulators will identify people who want to avoid repercussions from complaining about or standing up to abuse because they may fear the rejection that results. This trait is also known as Social Anxiety. Be careful that you are not intimidated into allowing people to violate your rights.

A lack of assertiveness or the inability to say no:

This trait is related to Social Anxiety, but it has more to do with your ability to set personal or professional boundaries and limits, rather than your ability to respond to the behavior of those around you.

A low degree of self-reliance or self-sufficiency:

Manipulators will look for people who need help because they represent a wide-open target for long-term victimization. Knowledge is power.

Absence of self-direction:

"Locus of control" is a term used to describe the degree to which someone is self-directed or whether they require the direction and control of some external authority or person to make decisions. People who tend toward having more of an external locus of control are more susceptible to emotional manipulation and exploitation.

Persistent naïveté:

Being trusting, innocent, and naïve is not in itself a negative character trait. However, the degree to which someone persists in the delusion that they cannot be harmed by predatory behavior, even when it has been made clear to them that they are being exploited and manipulated, can make it difficult to resolve instances of abuse.

Over-conscientiousness:

This trait is related to persistent naïveté. When someone knows they are in a manipulative or abusive relationship, an overly conscientious person may continue to give the abuser the benefit of the doubt.

Low levels of self-confidence or self-esteem:

People with little confidence are often singled out by manipulators because they will be more susceptible to flattery and deception out of desperation.

Over-intellectualization:

This is the mirror image of intellectual and bureaucratic bullying. For example, someone may be an obvious victim of bureaucratic bullying and continue to receive official communication promising resolution if the victim will continue to cooperate. If the victim over-intellectualizes the abuse by accepting the official-looking nature of the communication as proof of the predator's good intentions, then the exploitation will likely continue.

A dependent or submissive personality:

People who are naturally less assertive and who respond well to care, and love should not feel ashamed or that they are doing something wrong. However, a predator who identifies submissive personality types may successfully exploit such people without their being fully aware of the abuse. Often, the need for companionship and love may make otherwise shrewd and intelligent people uncharacteristically gullible and vulnerable.

Emotional and intellectual immaturity:

Immaturity, like naïveté, can result in a greater likelihood that people will believe exaggerated claims or promises.

Impressionability:

This trait is related to immaturity. Impressionable people may be susceptible to predatory abuse simply as a result of a charming or persuasive presentation or introduction.

Carelessness:

When honest people finally learn to adjust their responses to account for manipulators and predators, they may still run the risk of carelessness. Their newfound awareness of the treachery of the surrounding world may fill them with a sense of righteousness or entitlement—since they are not the predators or criminals, they should not be held responsible for changing their behavior. Although they may be right, failing to maintain vigilance after a real and present danger has been established can open the door to more abuse.

Narcissism:

Ironically, narcissists themselves can become victims of their own psychological deviance. Because of their obsessive need for flattery, they may be targeted by those who seek to disarm them using false flattery to gain their trust and respect.

Impulsiveness:

This is another trait that honest, naïve, and trusting people must learn to curtail. Although they may be right that they should not have to fear the constant presence of predatory manipulation, failing to conceal impulsiveness can leave them vulnerable to cons and other traps.

Altruism:

This trait is also respectable and admirable, but people who are overly altruistic and selfless become easy targets for predators who lack empathy.

Greed or materialism:

Negative personality traits can also make people susceptible to victimization. The contemporary environment celebrates materialism, greed, and consumerism. Because society has been engineered to make these attitudes acceptable and desirable, vast segments of the population have been set up as victims of financial criminals and other dishonest businesses run by people displaying the personality characteristics listed in the Dark Triad.

The elderly:

Elderly people are frequent targets of emotional manipulation. This applies especially to honest people who have maintained vigilance for a long period of time. Their success in having avoided victimization may give their confidence a boost, which may tempt them to let their guard down. In addition, the physical problems associated with aging may make them more fatigued and less able to maintain high levels of awareness.

CHAPTER 8
DARK PERSUASION

Whenever folks try to provide meaning to the notion of demeanor, their responses always come in various forms. Even though some could put their thoughts on the ads and advertisements which are everywhere in contemporary society, advocating you to patronize a specific product or service over the other others' heads fall back into the politicians. They attempt to modify the minds of Republicans simply to get yet another vote in the polls. Both instances are right since they are messages targeted at altering the understanding of this topic. The purpose of diversion between ordinary persuasion and dim persuasion is that dark persuasion doesn't necessarily have a moral rationale.

Even though a standard persuader might attempt to convince someone for this individual's own great, a dim persuader does so together with motives that are not always great for another individual. They attempt to obtain a total grasp of comprehension of the individual they would like to convince, and they take pains to do this since they exactly understand what the greatest motivation is.

While persuasion consistently has ethical consequences, a dim persuader doesn't concern themselves with those consequences. In reality, they are mindful of these but decide to put their eyes in their goal (s) rather than persuasion is a mental phenomenon in an individual's regular life. It's either that you're the person attempting to convince someone else or you're being persuaded. What makes the distinction between dark and ordinary is the motivation for this. In mass media, politics, legal and advertising conclusions, persuasion comes to play with all of the time. The results of instructing it in such areas are set by means of persuasion that will help determine the topic of persuasion.

There are a few clear and crucial differences between behavioral and other brain control varieties, like brainwashing and hypnosis. Even though these two demands that the topic ought to be isolated as a way to modify their thoughts and individuality, persuasion doesn't require isolation. To be able to reach the target, manipulation is utilized on a single individual. Although persuasion may also be performed on a single topic so as to make them change their thoughts, there's also a chance of using it on a huge scale to alter the heads of a complete group or a whole society.

Because of this, persuasion is a much better mind control procedure and maybe more harmful since it can alter the minds of lots of people at precisely the exact same time rather than the head of only one individual at one time. There are many people who make the error of believing that they have immunity to the consequences of persuasion since they are of the opinion that they will always have the ability to observe every sales pitch that comes in their way.

They think they'll always have the ability to use logic to acquire a grasp of what's happening and find a logical decision for this. As a result of how people aren't always likely to fall for whatever they hear if they utilize logic, so this might be accurate. It's likewise feasible to steer clear of persuasion since the debate doesn't augur well with the individual's beliefs, whatever the strength of this debate. But, some individuals understand how to use convincing messages to inspire people to market the newest gadgets or goods in the industry. This information action is quite delicate, so the topic won't always recognize it; therefore, it's going to be rather difficult for them to constantly have the ability to make an opinion regarding the information they will get.

Every time is said, it's extremely probable that you think about it in a terrible light. That is because they are inclined to automatically consider a conman or salesman who's always attempting to make them modify their view, and that will finally push them till this shift is reached. While black persuasion is notable in earnings and conning clinics, in addition, there are ways that persuasion may be used permanently, such as in diplomatic relationships between global bodies or at public service attempts. The difference only lies in the method by which in which the practice of persuasion is attracted to perform.

Dark Persuasion Methods

When an individual is prepared to modify the head of the topic by devoting them to do anything that's against their first frame of mind, the persuader will get some nicely laid out methods to assist them in reaching their targets. Every day that passes, the goal will face various kinds of persuasion. For food manufacturers, their aim is to receive their goal to test the recipes that are new or have them adhere to the past ones, even while studios may flaunt their most recent blockbuster films about the faces of the aims. In any situation may be whatever merchandise they're promoting, their principal intent is to generate more revenue, and that's the reason they're attempting to convince you. They couldn't care less about how this may affect you, and that is why they need to be quite careful and proficient in the art of subtle persuasion to make sure they don't deceive you off or make you plump.

As there are also lots of different brands attempting to convince you, they need to locate an exceptional approach to impress their perspectives on you. As a result of the effect of info on a vast selection of individuals, the methods used in it has been a topic of research for several decades, dating back to early times. That is only because influence is a really helpful instrument at the control of a large assortment of individuals. Beginning in the early 20th century, the proper analysis of those techniques started to grow. Bear in mind that the objective of attempting to convince people would be to push a compelling debate in an audience and have the positive.

They'll then internalize this information and embrace it as their fresh mindset or even means of life. Because of this, there's a fantastic need to find the very prosperous persuasion methods. Three dark persuasion methods have been shown to be of fantastic value through recent years.

Create a Need

This really is only one of the most profitable methods of obtaining an individual to change their perspective or lifestyle. The individual that's hoping to convince a goal will create demand or concentrate on a demand that the topic already has. If that is achieved in a suitable manner, it's the capacity of enticing a fantastic deal to your goal. This signifies that to be able to become prosperous, the persuader should interest the demands which are far more significant to the goal.

This could be their requirement to fulfill their own fantasies of fostering their self-esteem. It might also function as a desire for love, food, or shelter. This method will work out nicely since there's absolutely not any way the topic isn't likely to require one or more of these items or need anything at all. As there's absolutely no way, the goal is not likely to get dreams and ambitions. The persuader will probably and simply find strategies to produce the sufferer understand how they can easily help the sufferer attain those dreams. The persuader can also tell their goal the goal will probably recognize their visions if they make precise adjustments to their faith or outlook.

As stated by the persuader, doing this will provide the target a greater prospect of attaining success. For example, a young guy who wishes to get romantic with a woman may inform her that he'll help her boost her grades and eventually make her parents happy by obtaining A. Still, only when she's friends with him. However, this woman may believe she has finally discovered the salvation she desires. The simple truth is that the young guy is not very curious about how she fares in college; for the teenagers is just a lure for obtaining access to sexual activity.

Appealing to Social Needs

Another technique the persuader may utilize is identifying the goal of social demands. Even though this might not yield as many outcomes and the goal's main requirements will, it's still a significant instrument at the persuader's hands. There are those that are naturally attracted to audiences and want to feel desired. They always wish certain things, not because they want them but since it includes certain prestige. That makes them feel like they belong to a bigger course. The idea of appealing to your target's societal needs is what's accessible through several TV advertisements where audiences are invited to purchase a product. So, they won't be "left behind" When they could recognize and allure to the societal needs of their goal, the outcome is that they can achieve a new field of the goal's interest.

Making Use of Loaded Words and Images

When an individual is hoping to convince someone else, then they need to be cautious with their selection of words because words could make all of the difference. When there are lots of means to say something, one way of stating it might be more powerful than another. When it's related to persuasion, among the essential things is understanding how to say the ideal thing at the ideal moment. Words are the most significant tools in communicating and understanding the ideal call-to-action phrases.

Dark persuasion is just one of the most effective dim psychology theories, but regrettably, it's always overlooked and suppressed. This might be because, unlike many different head control procedures, persuasion renders the goal using a selection. At another mind control procedure, the aim is forced to enter. Occasionally this is achieved by placing them into isolation to ensure in conclusion. They don't have any say in the results of the procedure. In regards to persuasion, the chips have been laid bare (though with the ulterior purpose in dim persuasion), so the goal is made to make the choice they think will fit them best.

CHAPTER 9
BRAINWASHING

B rainwashing can simply be defined as a process where a person or a group of people make use of some underhand methods to talk someone into changing their will to that of the manipulator. When discussing this topic, it is important to delineate between honest persuasion and brainwashing, as there are several ways that people persuade one another these days, especially in the field of politics.

A very easy way that people persuade others to conform to their will is by stating a few things that could typically induce a yes response from the target. They then use some statement of facts as the icing on the cake. At the end, they state what it is that they want people to do. For example, consider the speech below: "Are you tired of paying exorbitant fares for your child's schooling? What about the rising prices of gas and power supply? Are you concerned about the constant riots and strikes? Well, a good point to recall that the government has mentioned the country is gradually drawing close to recession and that the prices of fuel will continue to rise as they are seeing the greatest drop in the economy since the end of the civil war. If you want the country to change for the better, vote democrats." The truth is that you may not want to agree with the fact that these are brainwashing techniques which may come off as subtle persuasion and that they are techniques in the hands of manipulators.

Some of the common manipulation techniques that you should watch out for include:

Isolation:

When trying to brainwash a person, one of the first things usually done is the isolation of the victim from their family, friends and loved ones. This is to ensure that the victim will not have any other person to talk to besides the manipulator. So, the victim will get all their ideas and information from the manipulator while avoiding any likelihood of a third party stepping in to ask what is going on.

Attack on the victim's self-esteem:

Since the manipulator has successfully isolated the victim, he must look for a way to break his will and self-esteem. They will then use the process to begin to rebuild the victim in whatever image they wish to. The only way a person can be brainwashed is if the person manipulating them is superior to them. This attack on the person's self-esteem would manifest in the form of intimidation, ridicule or mocking the victim.

Mental abuse:

The manipulator will try to brainwash their victim by putting them through a phase of mental torture. They will do this by telling lies to the victim and making them feel embarrassed by telling them the truth in front of other people. They can also bully these victims by badgering them and not leaving room for them to have any form of personal space.

Physical abuse:

Manipulators understand there are many physical techniques that can be used to brainwash the victim. These techniques include depriving the victim of sleep and making sure that they stay cold, hungry or causing bodily harm by exhibiting violent behavior towards them. The manipulator can also make use of some much subtler ways like increasing the noise levels, making sure that there is a light that is always flickering on and off or raising or lowering the room's temperature.

Playing repetitive music:

According to a study, if a person plays a beat repeatedly, especially a beat that has a range of about 45 to 72 beats each minute, it is possible to introduce an extremely hypnotic state. This is because repetition is much closer to the rhythm that comes from the beat of the heart of a human being. This rhythm, however, can cause an alteration to the consciousness of the person until they reach what is known as the Alpha state, which is where the person becomes 25 times more suggestible than he would ordinarily be when they are in a Beta state.

Allowing the victim to only have contact with other brainwashed people: When the manipulator is brainwashing a person, they ensure that the victim does not encounter any other person/people besides those that are already brainwashed. This is to create room for peer pressure. The truth is that everyone desires to be liked and accepted. This is more prevalent when a person is a new member of a group. In such a case, the person will typically adhere to and promote things that the other members are saying which will secure them a space with their new company.

Us vs. them:

This also has to do with the possibility of being accepted by a group. The manipulator makes the victim feel like there is an "us" and a "them." So, they are offering the victim a chance to choose the group they wish to belong to. This is done to gain absolute loyalty and obedience from the victim.

Love bombing:

This technique has to do with attracting the victim to the group through physical touch and by sharing some intimate thoughts with the victim. Emotional bonding is also used in this technique through a show of excessive affection as well as constant validation.

All the above mentioned are a few ways to brainwash a person. Once a person is brainwashed it is usually very difficult to get them back to normal. They develop more rigid neural pathways than other people and this could be an indication of why it is always very hard for a brainwashed person to double check their situation by rethinking it once they have been brainwashed.

CHAPTER 10
DARK NLP

The background of neuro-linguistics programming is that positive behaviors that lead to success can be copied. The professor and the student were interested in the difference between the thought patterns, behaviors, and language use of successful and unsuccessful people. Their findings are the basis of NLP today. Simply put, the researchers claimed that success has very little to do with luck. You do not have to be lucky to succeed. Changing your approaches to life can help you to become more successful in relationships, career, social situations, and other situations. Though some people develop natural ways of becoming successful. These ways of thinking, acting, and speaking can be learned by anyone who is willing to give it a shot.

The neuro-linguistics programming was developed years ago, but a lot of redefinition has taken place over the years. Currently, NLP has become a commonly used technique in self-development and therapy. It is used in education, business, military, and above all, for individuals. NLP can be successfully applied in your personal life, and a lot of big companies train their staff on how to use NLP with clients.

NLP is about how we develop mental representations, sounds, images, and verbal descriptions of different situations. When we become aware of the internal maps of reality within us, it becomes easier to consciously change our inner landscape and consequently respond differently to people and situations in the outside world.

One of the main benefits of using NLP is that results can be seen very quickly. For instance, people with some kinds of phobias can be treated in a matter of minutes using some of the techniques found in NLP. Furthermore, blockages and fears can be dealt with easily and quickly through the use of NLP. Honestly speaking, NLP has shed a lot of light on how we interact with our physical and social environments and other aspects of life.

Can NLP help you avoid negative manipulation and mind control? Yes, NLP can help anyone to fight manipulators. Often, we move along life on autopilot-responding to life in an extensively automatic way. This leaves us vulnerable to manipulation because we hardly analyze situations critically and make strong decisions. When living life on autopilot, we tend to follow what other people are doing (social proof) and allow other people to influence our choices. Sometimes we go through life driven by those subconscious programs which we have learned and practiced for years – some of them we practice since childhood.

Some self-development advocates and personal change ambassadors can fail to explain to us how we can avoid the specific tools we should apply to improve our lives. On the other hand, NLP lays out the tools you need to implement that change. It informs you that you are responsible for your actions, reactions, and responses to the situations in life. NLP allows you to get behind the steering wheel and take charge of your life instead of having another person drive you around.

NLP is practiced more because of its practicality – The tools are functional, and a wide range of challenges can be addressed through NLP. Some of the issues include:

- Developing better relationships

- Becoming more healthy

- Overcoming phobias and fears such as fear of public speaking

- Improving communication

- Being more successful and impactful in your career and family life.

Success in any field of life, be it career, sport, family, etc. requires excellence. Neuro Linguistic Programming is a roadmap for this excellence. Although other factors like luck and innate ability play a role in the success of an individual, the majority of NLP tools must be applied. Success is a predictable result of behaving and thinking in a certain way.

Manipulating the Mind with NLP

As you may already know, there are several techniques that can be employed when it comes to the subject of mind control. For the purpose of this book, in this section we are going to focus on the ways in which the mind can be manipulated with the use of NLP. The following are a few of those ways:

Close attention to the person:

When a person is trying to manipulate another person's mind with the use of NLP, they do so by first paying close attention to the subtle cues of the person like breathing pattern, body language, pupil dilation, eye movement, nervous tics, body flush and so on. Thanks to the fact that the emotions of a person at a time are easily linked to such cues, it is easy for the NLP user to infer the person's state of mind.

Talking with a suggestive frequency of the human mind:

This has to do with the uttering of words close to a person's heartbeat, which typically is about 42 to 72 beats every minute. When this is done, it can induce a high state of suggestibility to a person's mind.

Moving past the conscious mind with the use of voice roll:

This is a manipulating technique that has to do with voice roll, which is a patterned pace style that entrenches a desired point by skipping a person's conscious mind and going to the subconscious mind. An NLPer does this by placing emphasis on the word they desire the receiver to hear in a patterned style of monotony.

Building rapport easily, in secret:

This is a manipulative technique used by the skilled NLP user. It is done by employing language to boost suggestibility. To create a rapport with a person, the NLP professional examines the person closely and pretends to adopt the person's body language in a very subtle manner, thus making the person more vulnerable to everything the NLPer suggests.

Programming the mind in a sublime manner and creating an anchor:

This technique has to do with a process of creating an anchor in a person such that it becomes easy to put the person in a particular state of mind by simply tapping on the person or touching them in order to program the person's mind in a sublime manner.

Using hot words in an effective way:

NLP professionals can adopt a pattern of words that may seem normal on the surface, but in truth they are permissive and suggestive. There are some hot words that are connected to the senses, these are the ones that are more suggestive.

They include words like eventually, feel free, see this, means, hear this, now, because, as, etc.

These words are very potent in invoking a state of mind like experiencing, feeling, imagining, etc. It also creates the perception that the NLP user desires in the mind of a person. Also, they can make use of some vague words to control a person's thoughts.

An interpersonal subconscious mind programming:

By making use of the interpersonal strategy, the NLP user can say one thing, when they are planting something else in the subconscious mind of their subject.

CHAPTER 11
HYPNOSIS

As you work toward the ability to hypnotize people, keep in mind everything else that you have learned thus far. The minds of other people are absolutely sacred and should be treated as such. If you are going to be influencing other people, you should always make sure to do it ethically. Remember, just because hypnotizing someone for your own selfish gain is dangerous and not recommended does not mean that hypnosis itself is bad. In fact, hypnosis has gained massive traction lately. You see it used during labor, with women self-hypnotizing themselves in order to avoid the pain of labor, focusing through the contractions as a way to manage their own comfort. You see people using hypnosis for cessation of cigarettes or other unhealthy habits. You even see people using it to help them become more self-confident.

Ultimately, hypnosis has no shortage of usage or of people willing to try it. If you remember to keep your control of other people ethical and consensual, there is no harm in using these methods. However, you must always emphasize consent above all.

Nevertheless, it is time to delve into the mysterious world of hypnosis. We will go over a few positive uses of hypnosis, such as in labor and delivery, and finally, we will look over the steps on how to hypnotize someone else that is willing to be your subject. If all goes well, you will find that influencing other people is far easier than you may have thought.

How Hypnosis Works

Primarily, hypnosis works because it is cooperative—usually, one person is willingly being relaxed into a hypnotic state, and the hypnotist then encourages the thoughts and behaviors that are desired. In a therapeutic situation, this may look like encouraging the individual to no longer care about an ex that left or being able to resist those cravings of sugar and to exercise more.

Effectively, it allows for the implantation of thoughts in a consensual way. This means that the hypnotist is just the coach—they are there to guide the way through the subconscious to create the results that the individual that is being hypnotized wanted in the first place. The hypnotist effectively is able to manage to walk the individual through the steps of hypnosis, and in doing so, guides the individual to that state of extreme calmness.

Within the hypnotic state, it is often reported that the one being hypnotized is convinced that they are asleep. They are so deeply relaxed that they feel like they are entirely unaware of the world around them. However, that could not be further from the truth—when you are in a hypnotic state, you are actually incredibly aware and focused—but only on what the hypnotist is saying. If the hypnotist is guiding you through breathing practices to keep you calm, all you will focus on is what the hypnotist is saying. If the hypnotist happens to be using any sort of prop or focal object, you will focus on that. In being so incredibly focused on one particular moment or instance, you will find that you are able to be readily and easily influenced.

This primarily works because of the divide between the conscious and unconscious minds. While the two minds work together, the conscious mind acts like a sort of filter between what the unconscious mind is being exposed to and the mind itself. This means that the conscious is basically the guard dog of the mind, and if it interferes, you are not going to be able to get through to the more susceptible, impressionable unconscious, which is where suggestions are meant to go.

When you encourage the conscious mind to focus entirely on one object or action, whether breathing or the swinging of a pendulum, or anything else, you distract the conscious. Think of what happens if you throw a dog a piece of steak: They run after the steak and happily munch on that while you are free to move forward. Effectively, with hypnosis, you throw your conscious mind a steak by having it so incredibly focused on what is going on.

As this happens, the hypnotist then makes several suggestions. They will talk to the one being hypnotized, making sure that the unconscious mind is able to absorb and internalize all of those thoughts nicely in order to ensure that they do, in fact, become utilized and acted upon. Because the unconscious mind is going to be the one driving actions without the conscious paying attention, those behaviors become quite easy. They simply happen because the unconscious mind does it.

Remember how in NLP, you are actively recognizing that the unconscious mind is the one that controls everything? That is effectively what you are seeing here. Hypnosis, like NLP, will make sure that the unconscious mind is acting accordingly to ensure that the one being hypnotized is able to do what was desired.

Why Use Hypnosis?

Now, with that in mind, you may be wondering why people are so willing and ready to use hypnosis on themselves to the point that they would even pay other people to help them with the process in the first place. The answer is that hypnosis is incredibly powerful because the unconscious is incredibly powerful. It should be used precisely because it does allow people to tap into their unconscious minds to unlock all of the potential that they needed to utilize.

When you use hypnosis, you effectively are making sure that you can draw all of the benefits that your mind has to offer. It offers you benefits such as helping cope with any phobias or anxiety triggers that you may have. If your anxiety and phobia is rooted in your unconscious, what better way to treat it than to directly impact it? It can help with pain management without requiring medication, making it incredibly valuable for people that will need pain medication but may find that they are at an increased risk for addiction or abusing that medication if they have it. It can be used to fight stress as well, working as a sort of grounding method for the individual using it if they want to reach a state of relaxation.

It can also be used in more insidious ways—some people use hypnosis to control other people. It is commonly used in brainwashing in cults, for example, relying on the constant repetition of words or other methods that are designed to tap into the unconscious mind in some way, shape, or form.

This means that hypnosis can be dangerous for those who are particularly susceptible to its effects. Not everyone is, but a vast majority of people are quite susceptible, and this means that these people could be subtly and unknowingly controlled by strangers without ever realizing that it was happening in the first place.

Using Hypnosis

Ultimately, hypnosis happens in several different ways—some people utilize an utter bombardment of the senses in order to trigger that unconscious state, while others will lull people into it with gentle storytelling or guided meditations. Nevertheless, regardless of the method, the end result is the same: The other person ends up being controlled without being aware of it. We will stop and look at two simple methods of hypnosis that can be used to trigger trances, which can then be utilized to ensure that the one being hypnotized is entirely obedient.

Bombardment

Think of a time when you had a teacher or someone else that was extraordinarily boring when they spoke. Though unintentional, that is exactly what this sort of hypnosis accomplishes.

When you use bombardment, you are effectively creating a constant and steady stimulation that drones on to lull the other person into a trance. It could involve someone speaking rapidly in a flat voice or using someone's naturally unvaried voice in order to eventually bore the person into a trance. The brain struggles with processing the information when it is all constant and unending, which is exactly why it becomes so difficult to understand.

If you want to use this, then, you will want to start up a single topic and stick to it for the next several minutes, making your voice as flat as possible. You want to talk as much as possible during that time, not relenting at all, even when you see that the other person is beginning to lose focus. As the focus is lost, you can begin to talk directly to the unconscious mind, making suggestions and encouraging certain behaviors.

Nonverbal Hypnosis

Another method is quite similar but is done in complete silence. However, this one will require you to have rapport built with the individual that you are attempting to hypnotize, as you are going to need to tap into their tendency to mirror you if you want to be effective. When you use this method, you are going to make sure that they are following along with your own body language, and you will start to do something repetitive and rhythmic that is still subtle, expecting the other person to follow suit.

When you use this, you are effectively having the same relaxing effect that you have on an infant that calms down when swayed. Just as the newborn calms down to the motion, so too do adults, even though they may not even realize that they are still susceptible to actions like that.

Start by ensuring that you do have rapport with the other person. With that established, you want to actively mirror the other person for a while until you know that they are mirroring you back. From there, you will begin to use several motions back and forth in an attempt to sway the other person into a relaxed state. However, the key here is making sure that whatever you do, you are making it subtle and easily followed without it seeming to stand out at all when done around other people.

Perhaps you start by tilting your head back and forth ever so slightly. It does not have to be particularly obvious—just gently and subtly move your head in a rhythmic manner. Chances are, so long as you are subtle enough, the other person will never notice that you are doing it—but they will pick up on it themselves. As you do this, begin to use more of your body as well, but make sure it is still just as subtle. Perhaps you slowly raise and lower your shoulders ever so slightly along with the slight roll of your head. Then, perhaps you also make it a point to rock back and forth on your heels as well. You may also alter your breathing as well in an attempt to ensure that the other person is breathing deeply and calmly.

With some time and effort, you will find that the other person is following all of your cues, especially if you are a trusted party in the first place. As they begin to relax, you will find that they are far more susceptible to what you are saying, and you are more likely to be able to get them to internalize information in this state than before. Make sure that you tell them everything that you wanted their unconscious mind to know before you stop the hypnotic motions, otherwise you risk them coming out of the trance too early, mitigating everything that you are doing.

CHAPTER 12
BEHAVIORAL TRAITS OF FAVORITE VICTIMS
OF
MANIPULATORS

There are certain characteristics and behavioral traits that make people more vulnerable to manipulation, and people with dark psychology traits know this full well. They tend to seek out victims who have those specific behavioral traits because they are essentially easy targets. Let's discuss 6 of the traits of the favorite victims of manipulators.

Emotional insecurity and fragility

Manipulators like to target victims who are emotionally insecure or emotionally fragile. Unfortunately for these victims, such traits are very easy to identify even in total strangers, so it's easy for experienced manipulators to find them.

People who are emotionally insecure tend to be very defensive when they are attacked or when they are under pressure, and that makes them easy to spot in social situations. Even after just a few interactions, a manipulator can gauge with a certain degree of accuracy, how insecure a person is. They'll try to provoke their potential targets in a subtle way, and then wait to see how the targets react. If they are overly defensive, manipulators will take it as a sign of insecurity, and they will intensify their manipulative attacks.

Manipulators can also tell if a target is emotionally insecure if he/she redirects accusations or negative comments. They will find a way to put you on the spot, and if you try to throw it back at them, or to make excuses instead of confronting the situation head-on, the manipulator could conclude that you are insecure and therefore an easy target.

People who have social anxiety also tend to have emotional insecurity, and manipulators are aware of this fact. In social gatherings, they can easily spot individuals who have social anxiety, then target them for manipulation. "Pickup artists" are able to identify the girls who seem uneasy in social situations by the way they conduct themselves. Social anxiety is difficult to conceal, especially to manipulators who are experienced at preying on emotional vulnerability.

Emotional fragility is different from emotional insecurity. Emotionally insecure people tend to show it all the time, while emotionally fragile people appear to be normal, but they break down emotionally at the slightest provocation. Manipulators like targeting emotionally fragile people because it's very easy to elicit a reaction from them. Once a manipulator finds out that you are emotionally fragile, he is going to jump at the chance to manipulate you because he knows it would be fairly easy.

Emotional fragility can be temporary, so people with these traits are often targeted by opportunistic manipulators. A person may be emotionally stable most of the time, but he/she may experience emotional fragility when they are going through a breakup, when they are grieving, or when they are dealing with a situation that is emotionally draining. The more diabolical manipulators can earn your trust, bid their time, and wait for you to be emotionally fragile. Alternatively, they can use underhanded methods to induce emotional fragility in a person they are targeting.

Sensitive people

Highly sensitive people are those individuals who process information at a deeper level and are more aware of the subtleties in social dynamics. They have lots of positive attributes because they tend to be very considerate of others, and they watch their step to avoid causing people any harm, whether directly or indirectly. Such people tend to dislike any form of violence or cruelty, and they are easily upset by news reports about disastrous occurrences, or even depictions of gory scenes in movies.

Sensitive people also tend to get emotionally exhausted from taking in other people's feelings. When they walk into a room, they have the immediate ability to detect other people's moods, because they are naturally skilled at identifying and interpreting other people's body language cues, facial expressions, and tonal variations.

Manipulators like to target sensitive people because they are easy to manipulate. If you are sensitive to certain things, manipulators can use them against you. They will feign certain emotions to draw sensitive people in so that they can exploit them.

Sensitive people also tend to scare easily. They have a heightened "startle reflex," which means that they are more likely to show clear signs of fear or nervousness in potentially threatening situations. For example, sensitive people are more likely to jump up when someone sneaks up on them, even before they determine whether they are in any real danger. If you are a sensitive person, this trait can be very difficult to hide, and malicious people will be able to see it from a mile away.

Sensitive people also tend to be withdrawn. They are mostly introverts, and they like to keep to themselves because social stimulation can be emotionally draining for them. Manipulators who are looking to control others are more likely to target people who are introverted because that trait makes it easy to isolate potential victims.

Manipulators can also identify sensitive people by listening to how they talk. Sensitive people tend to be very proper; they never use vulgar language, and they tend to be very politically correct because they are trying to avoid offending anyone. They also tend to be polite, and they say please and thank you more often than others. Manipulators go after such people because they know that they are too polite to dismiss them right away; sensitive people will indulge anyone because they don't want to be rude, and that gives malicious people a way in.

Empathic people

Emphatic people are generally similar to highly sensitive people, except that they are more attuned to the feelings of others and the energy of the world around them. They tend to internalize other people's suffering to the point that it becomes their own. In fact, for some of them, it can be difficult to distinguish someone's discomfort from their own. Emphatic people make the best partners because they feel everything you feel. However, this makes them particularly easy to manipulate, which is why malicious people like to target them.

Malicious people can feign certain emotions, and convey those emotions to empathic people, who will feel them as though they were real. That opens them up for exploitation. Empathic people are the favorite targets of psychopathic con men because they feel so deeply for others. A con man can make up stories about financial difficulties and swindle lots of money from empathic people.

The problem with being empathic is that because you have such strong emotions, you easily dismiss your own doubts about people because you would much rather offer help to a person who turns out to be a lair than deny help to a person who turns out to be telling the truth.

Emphatic people have a big-hearts, and they tend to be extremely generous, often to their own detriment. They are highly charitable, and they feel guilty when others around them suffer, even if it's not their fault and they can't do anything about it. Malicious people have a very easy time taking such people on guilt trips. They are the kind of people who would willingly fork over their life savings to help their friends get out of debt, even if it means they would be ruined financially.

Malicious people like to get into relationships with emphatic people because they are easy to take advantage of. Emphatic people try to avoid getting into intimate relationships in the first place because they know that it's easy for them to get engulfed in such relationships and to lose their identities in the process. However, manipulators will doggedly pursue them because they know that once they get it, they can guilt the empathic person into doing anything they want.

Fear of loneliness

Many people are afraid of being alone, but this fear is more heightened in a small percentage of the population. This kind of fear can be truly paralyzing for those who experience it, and it can open them up to exploitation by malicious people. For example, there are many people who stay in dysfunctional relationships because they are afraid, they will never find someone else to love them if they break up with an abusive partner. Manipulators can identify this fear in a victim, and they'll often do everything they can to fuel it further to make sure that the person is crippled by it. People who are afraid of being alone can tolerate or even rationalize any kind of abuse.

The fear of being alone can be easy to spot in a potential victim. People with this kind of fear tend to exude some level of desperation at the beginning of relationships, and they can sometimes come across as clingy. While ordinary people may think of being clingy as a red flag, manipulative people will see it as an opportunity to exploit somebody. If you are attached to them, they'll use manipulative techniques to make you even more dependent on them. They can withhold love and affection (e.g., by using the silent treatment) to make the victim fear that he/she is about to get dumped so that they act out of desperation and cede more control to the manipulator.

The fear of being alone is, for the most part, a social construct, and it disproportionately affects women more than men. For generations, our society has taught women that their goal in life is to get married and have children, so, even the more progressive women who reject this social construct are still plagued by social pressures to adhere to those old standards. That being said, the fact is that men also tend to be afraid of being alone.

People with abandonment issues stemming from childhood tend to experience the fear of loneliness to a higher degree. There are also those people who may not necessarily fear loneliness in general, but they are afraid of being separated from the important people in their lives. For example, lots of people end up staying in abusive or dysfunctional relationships because they are afraid of being separated from their children.

Fear of disappointing others

We all feel a certain sense of obligation towards the people in our lives, but there are some people who are extremely afraid of disappointing others. This kind of fear is similar to the fear of embarrassment and the fear of rejection because it means that the person puts a lot of stock into how others perceive him or her. The fear of disappointing others can occur naturally, and it can actually be useful in some situations; parents who are afraid of disappointing their families will work harder to provide for them, and children who are afraid of disappointing their parents will study harder at school. In this case, the fear is actually constructive. However, it becomes unhealthy when it's directed at the wrong people, or when it forces you to compromise your own comfort and happiness.

When manipulators find out that you have a fear of disappointing others, they'll try to put you in a position where you feel like you owe them something. They'll do certain favors for you, and then they'll manipulate you into believing that you have a sense of obligation towards them. They will then guilt you into complying with any request whenever they want something from you.

CHAPTER 13
HOW TO PROTECT YOURSELF AGAINST DARK PSYCHOLOGY

With an understanding of warning signs of covert manipulation, you are in a position to learn how to arm yourself against such manipulative actions. There are several tactics you can use in order to disarm a manipulator and escape exploitation. Seek to employ these different tactics to disempowering manipulators any time you start detecting signs of intentional manipulation attempts. You may find yourself becoming a far less desirable target if you put up any sort of fight.

Recognize Your Rights

Though this is important in a civil sense of knowing your constitutional rights as well, this is a reference to human rights. Human rights are the rights that every person is deserving of simply by virtue of being human. By recognizing your rights, you will be able to protect them when you feel as though they are being infringed upon. Manipulation always infringes upon human rights, so knowing what your human rights are is the perfect way to judge this. Here are some of your most fundamental human rights, though there are others as well:

You deserve to be regarded with respect. Every human should be treated with human decency.

You are within your rights to express how you feel or what you want or think. This freedom to think means that you should be able to speak your mind without fear of repercussion.

You control your priorities and goals. You have the right to decide what to pursue or what to avoid.

You are within your rights to say no without guilt. You are not obligated to do anything you do not want to just because someone else tried to force it upon you.

You have the right to protect yourself from physical, mental, or emotional harm. You deserve to be taken care of physically, mentally, and emotionally.

You are within your rights to pursue a life that will bring you happiness.

These rights are typically going to be respected by most people, but manipulators do not care about them. The manipulators are thrilled to take away these rights in order to control you—in essence; you are nothing but an emotional slave to the manipulator. Ultimately, however, you are well within your rights to assert and enforce any of the above boundaries, as well as any other boundaries that make you comfortable, no matter how ridiculous other people may think they are.

Watch Closely

One of the most surefire ways to avoid being manipulated is to avoid manipulators themselves. This involves studying other people and how they interact with the world around them. If you identify someone who is behaving in a way that you believe is likely manipulative, staying away from this person is a good way to avoid the hassle altogether.

When you engage in this sort of people-watching, look for extreme shifts in behaviors. While we all have ways that we tweak our behaviors depending on the context, typically, manipulators are within extremes. They are either polite or horribly rude. They may be aggressive to one person while gentle and kind to another, depending on the context. People who so drastically swing from one mood to the next depending on the person should be kept at an arm's distance.

Look For Self-Blame And Counter It

Oftentimes, manipulators will instill self-blame and self-doubt within their targets. This is done by exploiting weaknesses and sensitivities. We all have moments of feeling like we are insufficient or unsatisfactory sometimes, however, if you notice that you begin to feel this way more frequently than usual, you should stop and seek to analyze why you are having those feelings. It may be time to reflect on whatever relationship you have with that particular person you associate with those feelings of inadequacy and determine whether the relationship is worth continuing. You may ask yourself if you are being respected within the relationship, or if current demands upon you are reasonable. The most important self-reflection, however, is that you should identify whether you feel good and comfortable within the relationship or if the relationship should continue.

Try Not To Surrender To Dangers

Manipulators love to make dangers. You can't enable the dangers to be effective, so defuse all dangers right away. I will consistently recollect seeing Bob gradually turn in his seat to call the CEO when Kmart's manipulator had undermined him.

Know The Realities

Prior to going into a gathering with the manipulator, make certain to get every one of the realities. Frequently Bob would have outlines and charts to present should the need emerge.

Make Them A Piece Of Groups, However With Limits

Incorporate manipulators in your extraordinary groups. In spite of the fact that they will probably accuse others when things turn out badly, they won't have the option to accuse the collaboration all in all - they are a piece of the group and no manipulator will ever point fault their very own way.

Have An Extraordinary Checking Framework

Sway was in steady contact with the entirety of his kin. We knew to share issues and mix-ups as quickly as time permits. We were certain when we did with the goal that he would turn into our promoter. We never feared retaliations.

Approach Them For Strong Subtleties

At the point when the manipulator makes claims for which you're ill-equipped, request whatever number subtleties as could be expected under the circumstances. Ordinarily the manipulator will have no subtleties accessible at all because of their regular act of talking without actualities. This will rapidly uncover their reasons.

Shift The Focus

Instead of giving in to whatever the manipulator demands, try shifting the focus back to the manipulator instead of allowing it to remain on you. You could ask if the manipulator thinks the assertions or requests seem reasonable or ask if you are going to get something out of the current arrangement. Considering that most manipulators go out of their way to avoid blame or detection, by returning the focus of the conversation back to them, you make yourself seem far less attractive as a potential target. The manipulator may instead withdraw any attempts to sway you and move on to someone else.

Use Time

Just as manipulators try to weaponize time, you too can use it to your advantage. Instead of pressing for a rushed decision, answer that you will consider it, but do not commit. You can remove yourself from the other person's manipulation attempt simply by taking the power back. With an assertion that you will think about it and answer later, there is no wiggle room for the manipulator to force your hand.

Say No—And Mean It

Some people struggle to say no to others. Particularly those with lower self-esteem may really struggle with such a feat. However, by learning how to say no without justifying yourself or your reasoning, and enforcing that particular decision, you are able to remove power from manipulators. Manipulators prey on people's inability to say no, or the discomfort of displeasing people, so if you master the art of saying no, you are no longer an attractive target. If the manipulator does try to push past the no or disrespect your decision and boundary, you are well within your rights to set some sort of consequence as well. After all, sometimes the only way someone learns is through consequences.

CHAPTER 14
HOW NOT TO BE MANIPULATED

At the end of the day, we are indeed humans. It's precisely because of this that we get to dwell on the view of others in everything we do. We always want and love validation from others so we can subconsciously decide whether or not we will be depressed. In this millennial age, the norm has been just bragging about their wealth in social media. Many of these bragging is often the reality but, in the end, this leads to a loose connection with reality. This kind of self-deception can dig deep into the human system, and one day a victim of this may wake up and realize that only in her servant's eye does her perfect world exist. Depression will follow suit tightly. The first step towards protecting yourself against persuasion and manipulation is to confront the scenario and to take the position of disrupting any illusions. You won't be able to go through your lives usually. You must be careful that you regulate your own decisions and then consciously decide to see stuff for what they really are. This agreement, which seems too good to be true, could actually be true. The other thing you should do is trust your instincts certainly. Sometimes you have been told a lie in the most competent manner that you can believe. But at a specific instinctive rate, you can feel an imbalance between what should, what is, and then what is projected on you. There might be no physical sign that something is wrong, but you think that something is wrong. The next significant thing when you ask questions is to hear the answers. This can sound unbelievable because you're going to listen to the responses. The reality is that we can deceive ourselves by choosing the responses we receive. We say that we look, but we only care about the reactions that we want to hear and not the answers that we receive. You may have broken your illusions, but some of you still hold on to the comfort of those illusions. You would not hear the real answers to your questions because of the pain that comes with handling the scenario. Actual hearing needs a certain feeling of detachment, but not reality this time around.

You must get rid of your feelings. Your detachment from your emotions would lead you to the next step in processing the new data logically. It can make situations more complicated than they have to be. It makes it so hard for your exit strategy, to allow all feelings to cool down and spring. The irrational part of you may want to let everything go to hell when you face reality. Your justified anger can encourage you to take short-term measures to calm your feelings. But you may come to regret these actions in the long term. I'm not saying that you should deny your emotions; I'm not saying that you do not act on these emotions. First, deal with the situations and later deal with your emotions.

Act Fast

It's lovely that you have gotten to grips with the truth of things. But it is so much more to defend ourselves against these dark, manipulative strategies. While you try to protect yourself against the claws of these manipulators, it is often intense and exciting at first. The intensity of these feelings can slowly lead to negation. The longer you take any action, the quicker the denial will begin, and if it occurs, there is a strong likelihood that you may fall back and end up being trapped on the same internet. You can avoid this by taking action as soon as you know someone is attempting to manipulate you. This can be done in the most natural way possible, as when informing a close friend about some facts of the specific scenario, all the events that will eventually lead you to liberty can be so started. You should understand that after choosing to behave, the fabric is made of sturdier material than glass. The illusion can work its way back to your core by using fragmented parts of your feelings to solve it. When a liar is caught in a lie, you may try to hire others to implement that lying if they think they no longer hold you. A disappointing partner with whom you broke stuff lately would attempt to use the other shared links in your lives to change your mind. You are going to need both your logic and instincts if you want to get out of this unscathed. While the reality is that when you find that you have always been lied to, you get emotionally scarred, so you are still left untouched by the scenario. However, priority should be provided to follow the path that enables you to go to this toxic condition without further harm. You're mentally all over the location. Rage, hurt, and disappointment are the tip of the iceberg. But you must logically believe. Keep your head above the water and warn yourself.

Get Assistance Quickly

When you are trapped in the manipulations of others, confusion is one of the feelings you would encounter. This will obscure your rational thinking and make you feel helpless. You could even question the truth of what you're currently facing. If you continue to have those doubts, it will lead to denial. You will likely want to say that you have the whole scenario wrong. You misunderstood specific stuff and came to the incorrect conclusion. Such thinking would lead back to the weapons of the manipulator. Resist the desire to accept a second opinion. In a health crisis, people go to another physician to get a second view. This is to clear any doubts about your first diagnosis and to confirm the best course of therapy for you.

Similarly, receiving an opinion from another person can assist you in discerning reality and your next steps. Just remember, it's better to go to someone who's proven to have your best interest at heart many times. The next step is to confront the perpetrator if you have the assistance that you need. I recommend you choose the scene or place for this. Select a location that provides you the upper hand. That would involve some cautious planning on your part. If the offender exists in the cyber world, especially if you have been swindled by the person, you must engage the police and the authorities concerned. Do some of your research to find out the truth. After you face the offender and take the measures you need to get out of the scenario, the healing method must begin rapidly. The extent and severity you have been harmed, manipulated, or abused do not matter. You have to be able to go through it and wait for your wounds to be "healed," rather than sitting on your bed and living the past.

Time would offer you sufficient distance from your experience, but you would seldom be healing from emotional scars if you learned something about this book. If you don't do anything, an unhealthy scab might form over the wound that makes you vulnerable, if not more than you have experienced. Speak to a consultant, take part in the treatment, and actively facilitate the healing process, regardless of what you choose. It will not occur overnight, but you are sure you get nearer each day with every phase of your treatment.

Have Confidence in Your Instincts

While your brain interprets signals based on facts, logic, and experience, it operates in the opposite direction by filtering data through an emotional filter. The only thing that takes vibrations is your intestine that cannot pick up either the heart or the brain. If you can groom up to the stage where you acknowledge your inner voice and are trained to do so, you will reduce your likelihood of becoming seduced by individuals who try to manipulate you. It's difficult to acknowledge this voice at first, and this is because we have permitted sounds of doubt, self-discrimination, and the loud voices of the critics within and without drowning our authentic voices in our lives. This voice or instinct relies on your survival. So, trust that your brain cells will still be able to process stuff in your immediate area when it starts. Some individuals call it intuition, some call it instinct, and they do the same, particularly when it comes to relationships. You must acknowledge that starting to trust your instincts may not always make logical sense. If you've ever been doing something and felt like you were suddenly watched, then you understand what I mean.

You have no eyes at the rear of your head, nobody else in the space, but you have the small shiver running down the back of your neck, and you're looking at the "sudden understanding", that is what I am talking about. I am talking about that. The first step in connecting with your instinct is to decode your mind with your voices. You can do this with meditation. Forget about chatting, concentrate on your middle. You're the voice that you understand. Next, be attentive to your ideas. Don't just throw away your head's eclectic monologue. Instead, go with the stream of thoughts.

Why do you believe in somebody somehow? How do you feel so deeply, even though you knew each other for only a few days? What's this nagging feeling about this other individual? You become more sensitive to your intuition as you explore your ideas and know when your instincts start and respond to them. You might have to learn to stop and believe if you are the individual who, at present, wants to make stimulating choices. This break provides you the chance to reflect and assess your options. The next part is hard, and many people can't follow it. You can't sail or navigate this step, unfortunately. You need to be open to the concept of self-confidence and trusting others to believe in your instinct. Your lack of confidence would only make you paranoid, and when you're paranoid, it's not your instincts that kick. It's your fear! Every molehill tends to transform fear into a mountain. You have to let go of your concern, embrace trust, and make your fresh relationships lead. You can hear the voice better without the roadblocks of fear in your mind. Finally, your priorities must be reassessed.

You may not see the past if your mind is at the forefront of money and material property. Any contact you have with individuals would be viewed as individuals who try to use you, and it will quickly become true if you live like this very often. Let's understand that we draw what we believe in, to your lives. If you always think about material wealth, you will only attract individuals like yourself. Look at your interactions with this new view with this guide; the old, the new, and the outlook. Don't enter into a partnership you expect to play. Be accessible to them, whether it is a company relationship, a romantic relationship, or even a regular knowledge. You can receive the correct feedback from your intuition. Do not think this too that, if you encounter suspects, your gut will tell you to go in the opposite direction.

CHAPTER 15
HOW TO CHANGE PEOPLE'S EMOTIONS THROUGH NLP

How NLP Works

If you are just coming across this topic for the first time, NLP may appear like magic or hypnosis. When a person is undergoing therapy, it digs deep into the unconscious mind of the patient and filters through different layers of beliefs. The person's approach or perception of life to deduce the early childhood experiences are responsible for a behavioral pattern.

In NLP, it is believed that everyone has the resources needed for positive changes in their own lives. The technique adopted here is meant to help in facilitating these changes.

Usually, when NLP is taught, it is done in a pyramidal structure. However, the most advanced techniques are left for those multi-thousand-dollar seminars.

Usually, the majority of NLPers are therapists and they are very likely to be well-meaning people. They achieved their aims by paying attention to those subtle cues like the movement of the eyes, flushing of the skin, dilation of the pupil, and subtle nervous tics. It is easy for an NLP user to quickly determine the following:

•   The side of the brain that a person predominantly uses.

•   The sense (smell, sight, etc.) that is more dominant in a person's brain.

•   The way the person's brain stores and makes use of information (the NLPer can deduce all this from the person's eye movement).

•   When they are telling a lie or concocting information.

When the NLP user has successfully gathered all this information, they begin to mimic the client in a slow and subtle manner by not only taking on their body language, but also by imitating their speech and mannerisms, so that they begin to talk with the language patterns that are aimed at targeting the primary senses of the client. They will typically fake the social cues that will easily make someone let their guard down so that they become very open and suggestible.

For example, when a person's sense of sight is their most dominant sense, the NLPer will use a language that is very laden with visual metaphors to speak with them. They will say things like: "do you see what I am talking about?" or "why not look at it this way?" For a person that has a more dominant sense of hearing, he will be approached with an auditory language like: "listen to me" or "I can hear where you're coming from."

To create a rapport, the NLPer mirrors the body language and the linguistic patterns of the other person. This rapport is a mental and physiological state which a human being gets into when they lose guard of their social senses. It is done when they begin to feel like the other person who they are conversing with is just like them.

Once the NLPer has achieved this rapport, they will take charge of the interaction by leading it in a mild and subtle manner. Thanks to the fact that they have already mirrored the other person, they will now begin to make some subtle changes in order to gain a certain influence on the behavior of the person. This is also combined with some similar subtle language patterns which lead to questions and a whole phase of some other techniques.

At this point, the NLPer will be able to tweak and twist the person to whichever direction they so desire. This only happens if the other person can't deduce that there is something going on because they assume everything that is occurring is happening organically or that they have given consent to everything.

What this means is that it is quite hard to make use of NLP to get other people to act out of character, but it can be used to get a person to give responses within their normal range of character.

At this point, what the NLP user seeks to do may be to either elicit or anchor. When they are eliciting, they make use of both leading and language to get the person to an emotional state of say, sadness. Once they can elicit this state, they can then lead it on with a physical cue by touching the other person's shoulder for example.

According to theory, whenever the NLP user touches the person's shoulder in the same manner, the same emotional state will resurface if they do it again. However, this is only made possible by the successful conditioning of the other person.

When undergoing NLP therapy, it is very possible for the therapist to adopt a content-free approach, which means the therapist can work effectively without taking a critical look at the problem or without even knowing about the problem at all. This means that there is room for privacy for the client as the therapist does not really need to be told about whichever event took place or whatever issue happened in the past.

Also, prior to the commencement of the therapy, there is an agreement that ensures that the therapist cannot disclose any information that means the interaction between the therapist and the client remains confidential.

In NLP, there is the belief in the need for the perfection of the nature of human creation, so every client is encouraged to recognize the sensitivity of the senses and make use of them in responding to specific problems. As a matter of fact, NLP also holds the belief that it is possible for the mind to find cures to diseases and sicknesses.

The techniques employed by NLP have to do with a noninvasive, medicine-free therapy that enables the client to find out new ways of handling emotional issues such as low self-esteem, lack of confidence, anxiety, and destructive relationship patterns. It is also a successful tool in effective bereavement counseling.

With its roots in the field of behavioral science, which was developed by Skinner, Pavlov, and Thorndike, NLP makes use of the combination physiology and the unconscious mind to bring about change in the thought process and ultimately the behavior of a person.

NLP Techniques

Here are some of the techniques that are employed in the users of NLP:

Dissociation

Everyone experiences a bad day when a situation ruins it and gives one a bad feeling. This may drown your spirit every time you are faced with it. Also, it may be a certain nervous feeling that comes at any point that you have to address an audience. It could be a feeling of shyness whenever you need to approach a certain (special) person.

Although it may seem as this feeling of shyness, sadness or nervousness is automatic and unstoppable, what the NLP technique of dissociation offers are ways to get over these feelings.

Get to know about the emotion that you wish to overcome especially when feeling of discomfort, anger, or dislike for a certain situation.

Imagine the possibility of teleportation and looking back at yourself going through the same situation, but this time from an observer's point of view. Take note of the dramatic change that occurs in the feelings.

To get an extra boost for your morale, think about floating out of your body and watching yourself. This means that you will now be looking at yourself while your other self is also looking at yourself. What this double dissociation attempts to do is to take away all the negative emotions in all possible minor situations.

Content Reframing

This technique is useful for all the times you feel like you are trapped in a negative or helpless situation. With the help of reframing, you will be able to get rid of all negative situations by becoming empowered by interpreting the meaning of the situation into becoming a positive thing.

Take a situation where your relationship ended, for instance. Although it may seem as if it is an awful situation when one looks at it on the surface, what about the possibility of those hidden benefits of being single? Think of the fact that you are now open to meeting and interacting with new people, which means that it is possible for you to get into a new relationship. This means that you are now free to do whatever you want to do at whatever time you want to do it. From the last relationship that ended, you must have learned some valuable lessons that will eventually be useful to you in your subsequent relationship(s).

It is very possible to panic or get thrown into fear in certain situations. Instead of focusing on fear, you can sway your focus by reframing. This will contribute to help you make some even-handed and responsible decisions.

Anchoring yourself

This process of creating a neurological connection between the ringing of a bell and the attitude of salivating is known as a conditioned response. These responses to stimulus anchors can also be used on humans.

The result of anchoring oneself is that a person gets to link a desired positive emotional response with a specific sensation or a phrase. When you can select a positive emotion or a thought and intentionally link it to a gesture, you will be able to trigger the anchor at every point you feel low, so you will be able to change your feelings immediately. Here are some ways of anchoring yourself:

Take note of the feelings you want to experience. It could be a feeling of happiness, confidence, calmness, etc. Decide on the part of your body where you would love to place the anchor. This could be a certain action like pulling your earlobe, squeezing your fingernail, or touching your knuckle. With this physical touch, you will be able to trigger the desired positive feeling whenever you want to. This has nothing to do with the part of the body that you have chosen, all that needs to be done is create that connection between the unique touch and the feelings. You do not have to make this touch for anything else besides the feeling.

Think about a certain time in the past when you had the same feelings you are experiencing at a given moment. Reminisce on the time you felt the same way then float into your body by looking through your eyes so that you will be able to replay and relive the memory.

Once done, you can make some adjustments to your body language to match with the memory and the state of mind. When you are reliving the memory, make sure you can see, hear, and feel everything the way you remember it. If you can do this, the feeling will come back, just as it will when you tell a funny story from the past to your friend.

CHAPTER 16
PREVENTING MANIPULATION

Manipulation normally occurs when an individual is used for the benefit of others. It is a situation where the manipulator comes up with an imbalance of power and goes ahead to exploit his victim just to serve their main agendas. Those who are manipulative are the kind of people who will disguise their own desires and interests as yours. They will undertake all they can to make you believe that their own opinions are the objective facts. They will then act as if they are cornered. Manipulators will pretend to offer assistance so that you can improve your attitude, performance, and promise that they will assist you in improving your life in general. That is all that they want you to believe. The hidden truth is that the main aim of these people is to control you, and not control you, as they want you to believe. They are not interested in making your life better, but just to change you. They also want to validate their lives and make sure that you don't outgrow them.

Once you have given these characters back to your life, getting rid of them will not be easy. They will appear to flip flop on issues and act so slippery when you want to hold them accountable. They also tend to promise you help that doesn't seem to be near.

People can be easily manipulated when they opt to put up with behaviors that are passive-aggressive. According to a recent study that was published in the Journal of Social & Personal Relationships, offensive people tend to interfere with the general performance of an individual. The study also noted that ignoring those who are negative could do you more harm than good. When these people are ignored, the research states that their productivity and intelligence is increased. More than 100 participants were examined for this study. The participants were asked to ignore or talk with random people who had been earlier asked to either be offensive or friendly.

The participants were not aware of the kind of people they were going to meet. After interacting for about four minutes, each of the participants was offered a thought exercise that needed them to have a better concentration. The study later noted that those who ignored the negative individuals performed much better than those who engaged the negative individuals.

The researchers then summarized that ignoring some people in a serious social interaction is one better way of conserving the mental resources of a person. The best strategy is to avoid those who are negative in their speeches and actions. But at times, that can't be enough. A negative person can also be manipulative and sneaky at times. In such situations, you will be forced to apply other strategies.

The truth is that being manipulated is not a good thing. The only possible worse thing than manipulation could just be admitting our dirty little secrets. Each time we realize that we have been manipulated, we not only feel stupid but also ashamed and weak. And all that doesn't stop there. If we continue to fall for the tricks that these people lay on us, they will leave us with an awful feeling about everything around us. Instead of being hurt for another time, the best thing to do could just be not to trust anybody.

Manipulation can only be successful if the target fails to recognize it or just decide to allow it. But regardless of all that, there exists certain things that you can do to recognize that you are under manipulative powers. They can also help you to prevent or stop a possible case of manipulation. Some of the ideas may not be desirable or possible for your situation, but that's just fine because every situation and every person is totally different.

Know all your fundamental rights

One of the single most imperative guidelines, when you are in this similar situation, is to know all your fundamental rights. But that's not all, you should also recognize when any of those rights are being violated. Remember that you are at liberty to stand up for yourself and make sure no single fundamental right is being violated. You should, however, do this carefully and make sure that you do not harm others. Again, you should not forget that you might forfeit these rights if you cause harm to other people. Ensure you are conversant with some of the basic human rights such as:

• The right to be treated with dignity and respect.

• The right to express one's wants, opinions, and feelings.

• The right to give no as an answer and maintain that without any guilty feelings.

• The right to set up one's own standards and priorities.

• The right to take care and safeguard yourself from being emotionally, mentally, or physically threatened.

The mentioned basic rights show the extent to which your boundaries are supposed to reach. We are living in a society where people don't represent any of these rights. The mental manipulators are particularly interested in depriving you of your rights so that they can fully control you and take advantage of you. However, you still have the moral authority and power to state that you are fully in charge of your life and not the manipulator.

Maintain a distance with these people

As noted, one of the surest ways of detecting a manipulator is to check if the individual acts with different faces when in front of various people and situations. Whereas all of us have mastered this art of social differentiation, the mental manipulators are masters when it comes to dwelling in extremes – where they show great humility to one person and rude to the other. They can also feel so aggressive at one point, and totally helpless the next minute. When you see this kind of behavior in people whom you are close to, the best thing to do is to keep a healthy distance. You should also try to avoid engaging with these people until you are really forced to do that. Remember that some of the top causes of chronic psychological manipulation are deep-seated and complex; therefore, saving or changing these people cannot be your job.

Stop Self-Blaming & Personalization

Given that the manipulator's agenda is to know where your weakness is and exploit it, you may even throw the blame game on yourself for not doing your best. In such situations, it is very imperative to reassure yourself that you are not part of the problem. Remember that you are just being manipulated to feel bad about your actions and surrender your rights and power in the end. It is vital to consider the kind of relationship you have with the manipulator as well. These are some of the questions that you should ask yourself:

•   Am I getting a respectful treatment?

•   Is this relationship 1-way or 2-way?

•   Am I satisfied being in this relationship?

The answers to these issues will offer you the most important clues about whether the problem is with the manipulator or with you.

Probe the Manipulators

Mental manipulators will always make demands or requests from you. They do this to make you go the extra mile so that you can meet their needs. At times, it can be very important to put the focus back on the manipulator each time you hear certain solicitations. Ask them some analytical questions to check if they are fully aware of their scheme's inequity. Ask them if their actions appear reasonable to them or if what they want from you is all fair.

When you step out to ask some of these questions, you are simply placing a mirror so the manipulator will be able to view the real nature of his/her ploy. If the manipulator happens to be a master of self-awareness, then he/she will definitely withdraw and back down. Real pathological manipulators, on the other hand, will dismiss the question and insist on having things done their own way. When this takes place, ensure you stand up for your fundamental rights and the manipulators will definitely flee.

Say No in a Firm and Diplomatic Way

Saying no in a firm and diplomatic way is what can be defined as real communication. When it has been articulated in an effective manner, it will give you an opportunity to stand your ground and maintain the best working relationship. It is important to remember that one of your basic human rights is to set your own standards and priorities. It is also within your rights to say no without feeling the guilt, as well as the right to pick your own healthy and happy life.

Set the Consequences

When a mental manipulator persists on violating the boundaries that you have made and is not hearing your "no," you will be forced to deploy the consequences. The ability to be able to point out and assert the consequences is one of the most important skills that you can deploy to resist the efforts of a manipulative person. When they are articulated in an effective manner, consequences will stop the actions of the manipulative person and even compel them to stop the violations and respect instead.

Confront the Bullies in a Safe Way

One fact that is not known to many is that a mental manipulator can turn into a bully when they intimidate and harm others. It is important to note that bullies only prey on those they regard as the weakest, and you can make yourself a target when you remain compliant and passive. However, the fact is that a number of bullies are cowards on the inside. They will often back down when their target starts to stand up for their rights. This is a common practice in office and surroundings, as well as in schoolyards.

Think about the long-term consequences of the actions you undertake

As opposed to just doing what is easiest and fastest, do not forget about the consequences that your actions can have. Remember that psychological manipulators are the best when it comes to making their option the easiest, fastest, and also the least hurtful. They are also best at keeping the people focused on their current feelings. That explains why people do things they later regret. Instead of dealing with a consequence later on, make sure you choose to do things that you won't be forced to rethink.

CHAPTER 17
THE EFFECTS AND IMPACT OF
DARK PSYCHOLOGY

With the little we now understand about dark psychology, we know that some personality characteristics linked to it are embedded in some of the most disturbing criminal offenses. This is, however, a larger side effect. I want you and me to get that closer to home. Why does this dark philosophy influence us... if it affects us? I can tell you there are no "ifs" to this problem and we'd explain it in just a few moments.

The attacker and the victim experience the results of dark psychology—we need to investigate certain aspects of obscure psychology to learn the impacts. Individuals that display such characteristics of personality that are considered enigmatic such as narcissism, psychopathy, and Machiavellianism, are likely to encounter problems in all facets of their relationships. When all three traits are present in one person, then they are more likely to commit a crime. The three-personality mentioned above traits have different features grouped under them.

For example, narcissism is characterized by a sense of entitlement, feelings of superiority deep seethed jealousy of others' success and exploitative behavior. Psychopathy includes an absence of conscience, an absence of empathy, destructive impulsive behavior, self-centeredness, and an inability to take responsibility as some of the symptoms. Machiavellian traits are signs of selfishness, ruthlessness, and manipulative behavior. These traits are worrisome when separated, but place them together, and they may spell trouble, particularly in the connection between an individual and others. For example, when the person is in the workplace:

- Underperform even the most sedentary duties in the workplace.

- Disrupts workflow because they can't get along with others.

- Other people would dislike them.

- Their impulsiveness will lead them to make questionable, non-ethical decisions.

- They are more likely to commit white-collar crimes if they are placed in an administrative capacity.

However, it is not just their relationships with the job that suffers. They are expected to experience the following problems in their personal relationships as well:

- Their intense need for recognition and affirmation for their partner can be overwhelming, resulting in faster relationship expiry dates.

- They exploit their partners, turning to physical and emotional blackmails.

- Their partners or children appear to be either mentally, emotionally, or physically abusive.

- Those who have ties with them are paying a high emotional price.

For the sake of your health and general well-being, if you have met a person whose relationships are marked by these encounters, stay clear of them. If, on the other hand, you are the one experiencing this, search out the therapeutic support you need to change. You can change your attitudes and perceptions with the right type of counseling, no matter how deep-rooted these issues are. The first step is to accept the situation for what it is, understand that you have a problem, and immediately seek assistance.

For the rest of us, it leaves us emotionally and mentally exhausted to deal with people who have the characteristics I described above. The impact can be painful at times, and catastrophic in serious cases. The poor neighbor whose horrible experience led me to write this book literally lost everything on this trip—her home, her career, but her loss was much deeper and greater than these. We had no connection with the act's perpetrator, but we still became victims. Our defeats have not been as dramatic as yours, but we have also felt defeat. We missed our nice neighbor, for example. She never died, but never recovered from the trauma. We lost our desire to confide in strangers. Also, our relationships with one another seemed to need an extra layer of confidence to succeed.

The biggest effect dark psychology has on anyone is that it has a deep sense of loss. We lose our valuables, we lose families, we lose ourselves (I'll explain that in a little bit), and they're sacrificing their lives for those that are incredibly unfortunate. Considering everything, it's fair to say the effect of this darkness is profound. If a person exhibits one of the dark personality traits, according to experts, there is a very high tendency the person would exhibit to the others. For general society, if the broader members of the community display these characteristics, it is fair to assume that there will be extremely high crime perpetration rates within that culture. This is not to suggest these people who live in towns or countries with higher crimes are more prone to criminality. Other factors contribute to consideration. Nonetheless, the risk cannot be ruled out completely either.

The ripple effect of behavior directly related to, or as a result of dark personality characteristics, is one thing that cannot be ruled out, though. Other negative habits turn victims into abusers as well, and this process continues long into the future before someone dares to break free and take the brave step. For example, more often than not, children from abusive families grow up to be abusers. In some situations, they find themselves stuck in similarly abusive relationships to break free from a parental mold even though they are not the abusers themselves. This is almost like feeling a very strong gravitational pull against the violent elements that dominated their home throughout their childhood.

For others, being victims may have such a profound effect on their psyche that it is causing something to crack inside them. I read; the "snapping" can be temporary. They lose all control over their innate instincts in a brief moment and act solely upon the greatest emotion that emerges that is typically rage. The disorder is what allows certain people to plead insanity temporarily. But some people accept the dark feelings as they 'break.' Any sense of morality is going out the window. The effects of that are typically catastrophic.

Day To Day Different Aspects of Dark Psychology Examples

When you think of dark psychology, you will be forgiven for assuming it just refers to any crime that lands you on the front page of the dailies or becomes a feature-length movie on the crime channel. It also involves quite a few items that have become widely socially acceptable, even though we do not personally condone such behavior. We see these acts in our homes, classrooms, workplaces, and now we see it on the internet, thanks to revolutionary technology. To help you get a better picture and hopefully a deeper understanding of this issue and tell you how close these acts are at home, I will share some of the most sensational crime news with you and the seemingly contradictory facts that lead to a horrible end.

First Case Study

News: A 14-year-old child brutally murdered

The Perpetrator's Traits: Dominant, Violent, Manipulative, Reclusive

Channel: Online Gaming

It was a young boy's sad tale of a well-rooted family. Any adolescent of the same age and social community had the same rights. He had a loving mom and a father who wanted to provide. The mother took all the measures that a mom will need to shield her boy from the internet's intrusive environment. Online gambling was just another thing that any teen should participate in. He will be fine as long as he has spent no more than the necessary time on it.

Yet there were dark plans for the suspect, who was just fourteen years old. A man manipulated the boy into visiting him at his place where he committed the heinous crime by deliberately exploiting his young and impressionable victim with lies. This had been one of the most disturbing events. Especially when you consider the victim's age and the perpetrator, regardless of his age, however, the attacker displayed many of the manipulative characteristics associated with dark psychology and snuffed out life just to gain power.

Second Case Study

News: Terrible case of domestic abuse

The Perpetrator's Traits: Physically Abusive, Manipulative, Controlling

Channel: Relationship

Love is a beautiful thing, indeed. You enter into a relationship with another, in the expectation that this person will love you and care about you—that you should watch for and support one another. It is you and the individual against the universe, in the language of modern love. And yes, this relationship started this way. A single mother who works hard to care for her son met this charming man who was exactly everything she had always hoped for in a guy.

He was sweet, compassionate, and seemed to love her boy just as much as he loved her. He left his job to make himself completely available for this young family and dedicated himself to caring for her until his true dark nature emerged. He exploited her using her love for the family in isolating herself from those nearest to her. He orchestrated the loss of her career, leading to the loss of her house. It meant she was utterly dependent on him. He moved her to his own apartment, where she was constantly subjected to torture around the clock, involving some of the most inhumane treatments.

His meticulous manipulation of the woman was so successful that when he gave her the option of how she wanted to be killed, she honestly mulled the thought about it as she felt she had no choice and did not deserve better. An opportunity and an act of bravery on her part contributed to the perpetrator's capture and imprisonment.

Third Case Study

News: A popular God minister accused of bullying underage leaders

The Perpetrator's Traits: Manipulative, egocentric, manipulating

Channel: Religious manipulation

The religious leaders have a special bond with their followers. The leader is supposed to be the moral compass, which guides the followers to lead their lives in the right way. For years, politicians have exploited their place of authority, irrespective of religion, opting instead to play the biblical reference to the current role of sheep and shepherd. And they prefer to be wolves, rather than shepherds.

This religious leader, having established his legitimacy by pretending to have direct contact with God, conned his members with his vision. At some point, he declared himself

Christ, saying that he had a mandate to sleep with seven virgins who happened to be minors too. He was later placed on trial and convicted of the crime.

These three cases are dramatic here, but the lesson to which I would like to draw your attention—such crimes were not spontaneous, motivated by the sort of evil that happened right now. This included meticulous orchestration that had groomed the victims until they hit and dragged them into the false state of trust and protection. In reality, how the events took place reminds of the role played by a predator and his prey. Next, there's stalking and watching the victim. Then, the predator makes a move based on the information acquired during the observation process. This step alone is not for attacking but for enticing their prey. Let them feel loved and well looked after. It is like wearing a mask and presenting characteristics they know relate to their victims.

Gradually trust is built up. The next goal is to make their prey dependent on them. The result is the same if it is either financial dependency, emotional dependency, or spiritual dependence. We want to feel important. Instead, they separate their prey and strike after it. You never presume or see such crimes coming a mile away. It is like a ritual of song and dance, giving the predator the upper hand and leaving the victim helpless.

CHAPTER 18
DANGERS OF DARK PSYCHOLOGY

Dark Psychology might be a new field of study, but the concept has been around far longer than even psychological researchers can pinpoint. They have discovered that everyone sits on the Dark Spectrum, some barely ever touching the dark sides of their brains, while others are completely immersed in it. On one hand, it's just like everything else in life, if you know that the possibility for these tendencies is there you will be better equipped to handle them if your mind begins to wander in that direction. At the same time, the idea that our brains have the capability to go that dark and deep into manipulative and dangerous behavior is frightening.

In everyday life, most people go through the motions, have goals, and set up pathways to their goals, and work to get there. There is no real thought of deception and manipulation. However, the fact that it sits so close to the surface will make you think twice about your decisions and others who make decisions that can negatively impact you. While you may not be worried about your own conscious behavior, you can't control the others around you.

The Dark Spectrum may be described as a line to some psychologists or like the petals on a flower to others, but either way, we all fall somewhere in that spectrum. It is vital to not only take a good look at yourself but at the people in your life as well. Where do they fall on this spectrum? What is their D-Factor? It may be something you've never thought about before but now brings some serious issues to mind.

Regardless of what the spectrum says, you are in control of your own behavior and decisions. You hold the key to just how dark you want to be. Maybe you enjoy the dark side of the force, but maybe it scares you, as it should. Manipulation and extreme deception are harmful, not just to you and to the aggressor but to society as a whole. We evolve with the times, and society dictates many of our actions.

Think about the last time you were under extreme stress. Think about the way you felt, some of the thoughts that circulated through your mind. Were you in total control of yourself? Did you find yourself slipping further down the spectrum? It's only natural to react to stress, anger, and negative emotion with an air of caution. But it's unfortunately also natural to want revenge. To want to take an easy route to the things we want in our lives. When we see an opportunity to have what we want, it's hard to turn away from that, even if it means putting someone else down in the process.

It's also important in times like those to think about what you are actually capable of. And if you believe you are capable of things nefarious and dark, ask yourself if you want to be that person. Those are the perfect time to reach out to people that care about you. Or reach out to a professional who can help you through these thoughts. There is no reason to give in to your dark psyche just because it's there. You want to be in control of your life, which means you don't want to control others or be controlled by someone else.

Once you have a really good grasp on your own level of capabilities, it is important to remember that not everyone is like you. From Ted Bundy to the guy who attempts to control you in a relationship, the spectrum is huge but real. If there was one Ted Bundy, there are more, hiding in someone's deep dark psyche. They may never bring him to light, but remember the possibilities are there.

None of this is said to frighten you or create a negative outlook on the world or other people. It is there to remind you that we are all capable of both light and dark. It is there to show you that Dark Psychology can be dangerous if used in the wrong way. So, keep your eyes open, be careful with the people you let in your life, and most importantly, take care of your own mental health. It is truly what can make or break your future. There are very few times we witness the bad guy truly win in the end.

Everyday Professions That Use Dark Psychology

We touched on the infinite depth that the dark psyche can go, but we've only lightly touched on the dark psychology used on an everyday basis all around us. There are numerous professions where people use these exact tactics to get what they want. Hopefully, if you are in one of these professions, you take heed and carefully tread as the dark psyche can often come back and bite you when you're least expecting it.

Lawyers

Lawyers use tactics of manipulation, deceit, lies, deception, and many others in their daily line of work. The entire point of their job is to convince others of someone's guilt or innocence. Often, it's a stretch to do that and they have to resort to these tactics in order to convince the judge or jury so they can get their way. There are a lot of examples of bribery within the judicial system as well.

Doctors

You may be thinking that doctors are there to help people not hurt them. And in most instances, this is true. But outside of actual diagnosis, there is a ring of pharmaceutical companies just itching for new clients. There is a reason that some doctors claim there is nothing good about natural medicine. It doesn't fill their pockets. Pharmaceutical companies bribe doctors all the time, pushing them to prescribe their medication to clients. This can easily lead to overmedicated people, people with the wrong medications, and a lack of quality healthcare for those that need it. It's definitely the last thing we need to worry about when we get sick.

Athletes

How many times have we heard stories of athletes being disqualified for things such as steroid and drug abuse? But inside the game, there can be some serious issues as well. Taking down other players to the point of injury just to win a game. Doing dishonest things like deflating balls is another. Within the realm of athletes, we've seen murders, abusers, and rapists arrested on a yearly basis. It makes you wonder whether the influx of dark psyche within the game has an effect on the dark psyches when they hang up their uniforms for the night and go home.

Police Officers

Between the beatings and the senseless killings, police officers are facing serious backlash from the community in recent years. Within the cycle of this type of job comes an extreme amount of power over people, their inability to hold that power at a reasonable level can be their dark psyches at work. There have been stories of murders, beatings, rapes, bribery, and deception within the police departments, but nothing ever seems to change.

Politicians

Did I really even need to list politicians? The list of Machiavellian style deceit, trickery, bribery, lies, deception, manipulation, and worse, inside of our political system, is outrageous. There are very few politicians in history that are clear from this type of judgment. They have twisted, jerked around, and manipulated the public for so long that most of us just try to pick the least evil out of them to support. Where money lies, so will a plethora of dark psyches. Politics seem to be a magnet for these types of people. There is power and there is money. What more could a dark psyche ask for?

Disturbing Dark Psychology Studies

In the 1960s, a psychologist by the name of Stanley Milgram began studying the psychology of obedience. It was not, and continues not to be, a highly researched area of psychology. In an attempt to study the human behavior behind the theory of obedience, he put together a study that looked more like an experiment of will. This study went on to be one of the most controversial pieces of research in psychological history.

Milgram took his volunteers to a lab where he explained that they would be participating in a study about learning. Each one was brought into the room one at a time and seated at a table with a microphone and a dial. The volunteers were then explained that there was, what he called, a 'learner' in the other room. They would be able to hear everything the learner did during this session. They were to ask the learner the pre-scripted questions they were given clearly and concisely using their microphones. At the time, the volunteers did not know the learner was actually a paid actor.

They were then told that if the learner gave them the wrong answer, listening to him through the speaker, they were to administer an electric shock. They would set the dial to the prescribed voltage and press the button. The dial was labeled from mild to fatal. During the process, an administrator stayed in the room with them, dressed in a white lab coat, looking like part of the team.

During the experiment, the learner began to give wrong answers to the questions that were being answered. Even when the volunteer hesitated, the administrator demanded that they continued to give the shocks to the learner, increasing the severity with each one. They could hear the learner's screams of pain through the speakers. If the volunteer refused, they were then instructed to continue with the following change of script:

- Please continue.

- The experiment requires that you continue.

- It is absolutely essential that you continue.

At that point, what would you do as a volunteer? During that experiment, a shocking sixty-five percent of the volunteers gave the learner the fatal shock. Even those that refused to do it, and demanded the experiment end immediately, never checked on whether the learner was okay or not. The problem was, they were fearful of the administrator. It was a cruel study but important to demonstrate the dark psyche's appearance in times of extreme duress. Milgram went on to use his studies to explain why the Nazi soldiers in World War 2 were so loyal to the cause.

The second study is equally as scary. Philip Zimbardo, in the 1970s, ran an experiment called the Stanford Prison Experiment. The entire premise of the experiment was to prove that people were manipulated into behaving in evil or scary ways very easily. A group of University students volunteered for the experiment and the basement of the University was made to look and feel like a real prison. Randomly, people were chosen to either be guards or inmates. While the study never fully revealed what happened in the basement, the study was cut from a two-week-long study to only six days. It was later said that the guards began acting in sadistic manners, only to find that they were completely appalled at themselves when the project was pulled.

CONCLUSION

Dark psychology tactics are all over the place, not just in psychopaths and murderers—just think of stereotypes associated with the used car salesman. They are charming, enthusiastic, and persuasive, all so they can get a sale out of you. From their job, they learn a bit about how to lead people on, exaggerate and persuade—their livelihood depends on this, so they get good at it. Of course, not all used car salesmen are like this, but having some dark personality traits certainly helps.

Manipulative predators capitalize on transferring their misfortune to other victims. They don't want to be alone in their unfortunate circumstances. Thus, they work tirelessly to ensure that they incorporate a few victims into their misfortune. If you soften your stand towards their cunning behaviors, you'll likely get incorporated into their sinister moves. You'll only find out when it is too late, and the repercussions are way too much to handle. For the manipulators, that will be a success in their advances. Their manipulation tactics will have already made an impact on the lives of unsuspecting victims.

Don't let someone ruin your day because they have an unsuccessful adventure. Such negativity can affect how you go about your daily business. It also reduces your morale when sorting out certain life problems. You ought to be in a positive mood to conquer your day to day ventures.

Hence, be brave enough to face your problems head-on. Don't let the manipulative predator's prawn on your ideologies and convince you otherwise. Also, be firm on the decisions you make. Most manipulators often notice when you are divided when making certain important decisions. They thus try to talk you out with the goal of ensuring that you change your perception. Besides, they'll try to create a bad picture of what you think is workable in your situation.

Good luck.

BOOK 2

HOW TO ANALYZE PEOPLE THROUGH PSYCHOLOGY

11 Practical Techniques to Speed-Reading People Like the Experts. Learn Body Language, Facial Expression and Body Mirroring to Improve Your Empathy with Other People

JASON ART

INTRODUCTION

Many people are inclined to the belief that understanding people and what they want is difficult. The fact that humans are capable of hiding their true intentions and thoughts supports this ideology, but only to a small degree. The truth is that human beings are the easiest to analyze due to the simple fact that we all tend to gravitate towards the same things.

In this book, we will go over some of the most powerful systems of personality analysis so that you can learn the skills that matter when it comes to mastering human psychology. With practice, you will be able to read people as the words on this page - and reap the benefits of having insight into people's thoughts and emotions. You will be able to improve your relationships and develop your powers of influence and persuasion by mastering this subtle but profound art of observation.

If you ask most people what they would like to achieve most in this life, the following answers will be prevalent:

- Money

- Career development

- Talent growth

- Happiness

- Prestige

- Peace etc.

We are all looking out for ourselves amidst a world with limited resources. The reason why you get up every day to work or study is all in an attempt to find your place in society and the world, and you must realize that everyone is in the same race. Therefore, before you attempt to study or analyze someone, you must keep the following factors in mind:

There are many factors to consider when assimilating signs from another person. However, two rules should be considered; cluster reading, which means gestures are analyzed in groups as opposed to being done separately. The other main factor is that the context must be considered too and not read in isolation.

Reading Clusters of Gestures Rather on Individuals

No-one is likely to be sending out singular signals because our brains are sophisticated enough to take in more than one clue consecutively. You might not even realize that you're doing it, but something does not ring true, so you start to look for as many signs that you can use to confirm or deny what you think is going on.

For example, when you think someone might be lying to you, don't just listen to what is coming out of their mouth but try to detect if their body language confirms or negates what they say. Below are a few suggestions that someone might be lying to you. In time, and with practice, you will be able to detect if someone is not telling the truth by knowing what signs to look for.

Looking up (trying to make up their story as they go along)

Covering their mouth (Can they believe what they are saying?)

Pauses (Don't know what to say next)

Blushing (I can't believe I said that, I'm sure they must know I'm lying)

It could be that someone uses something unique to them, but it is out of character, so it makes you sit up and notice. You then must draw on whatever other information is available to you.

A liar doesn't have to be lying maliciously either. It may well be that you ask a friend how they are, though they answer that they are feeling good, their body language tells you the exact opposite of what they've just told you. Look for corroborative evidence and never conclude on a clue, unless it's completely irrefutable. And even then, you might have misinterpreted it.

We are not usually consciously aware that we have so many clues coming at us to inform us about what is going on around us. But after being armed with this knowledge consciously, you can begin to look more closely for the clues and become more aware. The more you practice it, the more consciously you'll recognize the signs.

If you're trying to establish if someone is romantically interested in you and finally get them to go out for a drink with you, how does the evening progress? Are they mirroring your body language for instance? Which way are their feet pointing? If it's towards the door, then they're getting ready to run through it. Are they making eye contact with you? If not, they might be bored rigid. Are they laughing at your jokes? Or just smiling politely? Was that an eye roll? What more information do you need? Not everyone is going to think you're irresistible, even when you put your best foot forward, so you might as well cut your losses.

Unless, of course, you're confident you can turn things around and make them fall at your feet. Be honest with yourself. And face the facts. Write this one up as a practice or experience and move onto the next one. You're getting better and learning more each time.

Suppose you want to find out how your child's day has gone. How do you elicit more from them than 'fine' or 'okay'? Well, look at their body language and refuse to take what they are saying at face value. It helps if you can be casual about this and sit facing them so that you can mirror their body language and facial expressions. Try and present a relaxed stance and make sure your body language is open: open arms, uncrossed legs; make eye contact. If you do this, it helps them to feel that you're empathic instead of being judgmental. If you do persuade them to open up, try your best not to interrupt them. This is about them, not how you feel about it. If you start condemning them now, you might lose any future opportunity of discussion with your young person.

Only very rarely, do people say what they mean. It often needs more exploration that might be as simple as looking at their body language or noting it and following it up with a conversation. If you're alert, your relationships should improve in leaps and bounds.

Searching for Consistency

If you have ever observed a person taking a lie-detector test, you will realize that the interviewer always begins by asking questions such as:

Is your name Jane?

Are you Female?

Are you wearing a red shirt?

Is today Monday?

These questions are those that a person has no business lying, and they are used to identify the baseline i.e., how a person behaves when they are relaxed and telling the truth. Most employment interviewers also begin by asking similar questions, and it helps them establish the baseline of both verbal and non-verbal cues. That way, when they move into the more intense questions, they can be able to detect changes in demeanor.

When you meet any person you wish to analyze, you must be intent on getting the baseline from the word go. Regardless of whether you are meeting a person for a date or a potential working relationship, it is imperative to know their baseline actions. Otherwise, you will have a lot of trouble analyzing them.

This book is intended to help you gain a clearer perspective on your behaviors and patterns. This is something which can become tremendously useful insofar as helping you watch your gestures and mannerisms. This will allow you to convey the right message that you want to send to your interlocutors. You will not risk sending the wrong message, or mixed signals when you communicate with other folks.

So, let's get down to business. I am sure that you will find the information in this book to be useful and informative. You won't have to go searching for various books on the subject and combing through the Internet on websites that are littered with sales pitches and other gimmicks.

CHAPTER 1
BODY LANGUAGES AND VOICE BASICS

Do you know that people communicate much more through what they leave unspoken than what they say? Body language accounts for around 55 percent of the entire message during the process of communication. In a study conducted by Dr. Albert Mehrabian, it revealed that only 7 percent of our message is communicated through words, while 38 percent and 55 percent is conveyed through non-verbal elements such as vocal factors and body language, respectively.

Generally, what people say is well-thought and constructed within their conscious mind. This makes it easier to manipulate or fake words for creating the desired impression. Our body language, on the other hand, is guided by more involuntary movements of the subconscious mind. It is near impossible to fake subconsciously driven actions that we aren't even aware of. When you train yourself to look for non-verbal clues, you understand an individual's thoughts, feelings, actions, and more at a deeper, subconscious level. Try controlling the thoughts held within your subconscious mind and you'll know what I am saying.

People are perpetually sending subconscious signals and clues while interacting with us, a majority of which we miss because we are conditioned to focus on their words. Since primitive times, humans communicated through the power of gestures, symbols, expressions, and more in the absence of a coherent language. You have the power to influence and persuade people through the use of body language on a deeply subconscious level since it's so instinctive and reflex driven.

Here are some of the most powerful body language decoding secrets that will help you unlock hidden clues held in the subconscious mind, and read people more effectively.

Establish a Behavior Baseline

Create a baseline for understanding a person's behavior if you want to read him or her more effectively. This is especially true when you are meeting people for the first time, and want to guard against forming inaccurate conclusions about people's behavior. Establishing a baseline guards you against misreading people by making sweeping judgments about their personality, feelings, and behavior.

Establishing a baseline is nothing but determining the baseline personality of an individual based on which you can read the person more effectively rather than making generic readings based on body language. For instance, if a person is more active, fast-thinking, and impatient by nature, they will want to get a lot of things done quickly.

They may fidget with their hands or objects, tap their feet or appear restless. If you don't establish a baseline for their behavior, you may mistake their mental energy for nervousness or disinterest, since the clues are almost similar. You would mistakenly believe the person is anxious when he/she is hyperactive.

Observe and tune in to an individual completely to understand their baseline. This helps you examine both verbal and non-verbal clues in a context. How does a person generally react in the given situation? What is their fundamental personality? How do they communicate with other people? What type of words do they generally use? Are they essentially confident or unsure by nature?

When you know how they normally behave, you'll be able to catch a mismatch in their baseline and unusual behavior, which will make the reading even more effective.

Look For a Cluster of Clues

One of the biggest mistakes people make while analyzing others through non-verbal clues is looking for isolated or standalone clues instead of a bunch of clues. Your chances of reading a person accurately increase when you look at several clues that point to a single direction rather than making sweeping conclusions based on isolated clues. For instance, let us say you've read in a book about body language that people who resort to deception or aren't speaking the truth don't look a person directly in the eye.

However, it can also be a sign of being low on confidence or possessing low self-esteem. Similarly, a person may not be looking at your while speaking because he/she is directly facing discomfort causing sunlight. You ignore all other signs that point to the fact that the person is speaking the truth or is confident (a firm handshake, relaxed posture, etc.) and only choose to look at the single clue that he/she isn't maintaining eye contact to inaccurately conclude that the person is lying. Look for at least 3-4 clues to conclude. Don't make sporadic conclusions about how a person is thinking or feeling based on single clues.

For all, you know a person may be moving in another direction, not because they aren't interested in what you are speaking about or looking to escape, but because their seat is uncomfortable.

If you think the person is disinterested, look for other clues such as their expressions, gestures, eyes, and more to make more accurate conclusions. Include a wider number of nonverbal clues to make the analysis more accurate.

Look at the Context, Setting, and Culture

Some body language clues are universal – think, smile, or eye contact. These signals more or less mean the same across cultures. However, some non-verbal communication signals may have different connotations across diverse cultures.

For example, being gregarious and expressive is seen as common in Italian culture. People speak loudly, animatedly gesticulate with their hands, and are generally more expressive.

However, someone from England may decipher this behavior as massively exaggerated or a sign of nervousness. Enthusiasm, delight, and excitement are expressed more subtly in England. For the Italian, this retrained behavior may signify disinterest. While the thumbs-up is a gesture of good luck in the west, in certain Middle Eastern cultures it is viewed as rude. If you are doing business with people from across the world, understanding cultural differences before reading people is vital.

Similarly, consider a setting before making sweeping conclusions through non-verbal signs such as body language. For example, a person may display drastically different behavior when he's at work among co-workers, at the bar, and during a job interview. The setting and atmosphere of a job interview may make an otherwise confident person nervous.

Head and Face

People are most likely experiencing a sense of discomfort when they raise or arch their eyebrows. The facial muscles also begin twitching when they are hiding something or lying. These are micro-expressions that are hard to manipulate since they happen in split seconds and are subconscious involuntary actions.

Maintaining eye contact can be a sign of both honesty and intimidation/aggression. On the other hand, constantly shifting your gaze can be a non-verbal clue of deceit.

The adage that one's eyes are a window into their soul is true. People who don't look into your eyes while speaking may not be very trustworthy. Similarly, a shifting gaze can indicate nervousness.

The human eye movements are closely linked with brain regions that perform specific functions. Hence, when we think (depending on what or how we are thinking), our eyes move in a clear direction. For example, when a person is asked for details that he/she is retrieving from memory, their eyes will move in the upper left direction. Similarly, when someone is constructing information (or making up stories) instead of recalling it from memory, their eyes will shift to the upper right direction. The exact opposite is true for left-handed folks. When people try to recall information from memory, their eyes shift to the upper left, whereas when they try to create facts, the eyes move towards the upper left corner. A person who is making fictitious sounds or talking about a conversation that didn't happen, their eyes will move to the lateral left.

When there's an inner dilemma or conflict, a person's eyes will dart towards their left collarbone. This is an indication of an inner dialogue when a person is stuck between two choices. Increased eye movement from one side to another can signal deception. Again, look for a cluster of clues rather than simply analyzing people based on their eye movements.

Expanded pupils or increased blinking is a huge sign of attraction, desire, and lust. A person may also display these clues when they are interested in what you are saying. If a person sizes you up by looking at you in an upward and downward direction, they are most likely considering your potential as a sexual mate or rival. Similarly, looking at a person from head to toe can also be a sign of intimidation or dominance.

When you are observing a person's face, learn to watch out for micro expressions that are a direct involuntary response based on feelings and thoughts. These reactions are so instinctive and happen in microseconds that they are impossible to fake. For example, when a person is lying, their mouth slants for a few microseconds, and the eyes slightly roll.

How can you tell apart a genuine smile from a fake one? Pay close attention to the region around the person's eyes. If someone is genuinely happy, their smile invariably reaches their eye and causes the skin around the eyes to crinkle slightly. There are folds around the corner of the person's eyes if they are genuinely happy. Another clear sign of a genuine smile is a crow's feet formation just under the person's eyes. A smile is often used by people to hide their true feelings and emotions. It is near impossible to fake a smile (which is so involuntary and subconscious driven).

Even the direction of a person's chin can reveal a lot about their thoughts or personality. If their chin is jutting out, he/she may be stubborn or obstinate about their stand.

Posture

When a person maintains an upright, well-aligned, and relaxed posture, he/she is most likely in control of their thoughts and feelings and is confident/self-assured. Their shoulders don't slouch awkwardly, and the overall posture doesn't sag. On the other hand, a sagging posture can be a sign of low self-esteem or confidence. It can also mean placing yourself below others or subconsciously begging for sympathy.

When a person occupies too much space physically by sitting with their legs apart or broadening their shoulders, they are establishing their dominance or power by occupying more physical space.

Limbs

Pay close attention to people's limb movements when you are reading them. When a person is bored, disinterested, and nervous, or frustrated, they will fidget with an object or their fingers. Crossing arms is a big signal of being, closed, suspicious, uninspired, or in disagreement with what you are saying. The person isn't receptive to what you are speaking about.

If you want to get the person to listen to what you are saying, open them up subconsciously first by changing the topic of conversation. Once they are in a more receptive state of mind, resume the topic. When a person crosses their arms or legs, they are less likely to absorb or be persuaded by what you say.

A person's handshake can reveal a great deal about what they think about themselves or their equation with the other person. For instance, a weak handshake is a sign of nervousness, low self-esteem, and lack of confidence, submissiveness, and uncertainty. Similarly, a crushing handshake can be an indication of dominance or aggressiveness. A firm handshake implies self-confidence and a sense of self-assuredness.

Observe the direction in which a person's feet are pointed. If they are pointed in your direction, it means the person is interested in what you are saying. On the other hand, if they are pointed away from you, the person is looking for an escape route. Feet pointing in your direction or leaning slightly towards you are huge non-verbal signals of attraction.

CHAPTER 2
THE CLUE TO REVEALING TRUE INTENTIONS – EYES

The eyes are the windows to our soul—don't you agree? When we see a person for the first time, our gaze automatically goes to their eyes—looking, searching, and wondering who this person is.

In all honesty, it is easier to evaluate a person's heart than their mind. We can effortlessly pick up on our friend's mood or sense why our partner has dismissed plans to meet even without them speaking a word. How do we know this? How do we know what is going on in their heads without even speaking a word to them? For close friends, our partners, brothers, sisters, and family members—we just know simply because we grew up with them or because we've known them for a considerable amount of time to know what floats their boat, so to speak.

But how do we get this special access to the human mind towards acquaintances or your colleagues? Recent research tells us that looking at people's eyes is one of the ways to get in touch with the human mind, hence the phrase "I can see it in your eyes." It is poetic, and that's why you see it in so many music lyrics. While it's all beautiful and romantic, the truth is that the eyes can tell a lot about a person because while people can somehow hide their emotions and check their body language, they can't change the way their eyes behave.

How Does the Language of the Eyes Work?

When studying a person by looking in their eyes, firstly you need to do is subtly and not stare into their eyes. You need to maintain eye contact in a friendly manner and when you have established this, look into the changes in the pupil size.

A popular study published in 1960 says that the wideness or narrowness of pupils reflects how certain information is processed and how the viewer finds it relevant. The experiment was conducted by psychologists Polt and Hess from the University of Chicago, who analyzed both female and male participants when they looked at semi-nude images of both sexes. The study showed that female participants' pupil sizes increased in response when they viewed images of men and for the male participants, the pupil sizes increased when they viewed images of women.

Hess and Polt in subsequent studies also found that homosexual participants looking at semi-nude images of men (but not of women) also had larger pupils. This is no surprise at all because pupils also reflect how aroused we are. Women's pupils responded to images of mothers holding babies. This goes to show that pupil sizes do not reflect how aroused we are but also how we find a piece of information relevant and interesting.

This idea was brought forward by Daniel Kahneman who led a study in 1966. Kahneman is now a Nobel-prize winning psychologist. His study required participants to remember several three to seven-digit numbers and participants were to recall it back after two seconds. The longer the string of digits was, the larger their pupil sizes increased which also suggested that pupil size was also related to the information that the brain processing.

In looking for clues in the eyes of a person, the first step is to know what that person is thinking and to look deeply in their eyes.

Apart from the processing of crude information, our eyes can also send more sensitive signals that other people can pick up, especially if they are extremely intuitive. Another study conducted by David Lee began by showing participants images of other people's eyes and he asked them to determine what kind of emotions this person was experiencing. This researcher from the University of Colorado found that participants could correctly gauge the emotions whether it was anger or fear or sadness just by looking at the eyes.

he eyes also can reveal much more complex phenomena such as whether a person is telling the truth or if they are lying. For example, Andrea Webb conducted a study in 2009 which had one group of participants steal $20 from a secretary's purse and another control group was asked not to steal anything. This research led by The Webb and her colleagues from the University of Utah showed that pupil dilation gave away the thief. All participants were asked to deny the theft and the analysis of pupil dilation showed that participants who lied had pupils that were one larger by one millimeter compared to the pupils of participants who did not steal.

Our eyes also can become a good indicator of what people like. To learn to read the signs, you would need to look at the size of the pupil as well the direction of the gaze. Take for example someone choosing what they would like to eat at a restaurant. We are visual creatures anyway so our eyes are most likely darting between choosing the salad or the cheeseburger.

The other point to look into his decision making. When we are making a difficult decision, our eyes tend to switch back and forth between the different options in front of us and our gaze ends at the option that we have chosen. By observing these little details of where someone is looking, we can identify which options they choose.

Another way of studying this type of difficult trade-off is by offering monetary bets to participants. A study conducted at Brown University by James Cavanagh was when participants were asked questions that involved difficult tradeoffs between probabilities and payoffs.

Participants were paid based on their decisions. The researchers were kind that the harder the decisions were, the more the pupils of the participants dilated. As the choices got harder, our pupils also got bigger.

The eyes also give away clues as to if we experienced something unpleasant. Another study on eyes and their reaction was conducted at the University of Washington in 1999. The painful stimulation was administered to the fingers of 20 participants and they were asked to rate this pain from tolerable to intolerable. The more intolerable the circumstances were, the larger the pupils of the participants became.

Although pain is a very different feeling than looking at images of seminude people, it still showed a change in pupil response. This shows that pupil size correlated with the strength of feelings and whether those feelings were positive or negative. So if you want to know whether a person is feeling bad or good, consider the context and look into their eyes.

So What Does This Mean in Terms of Non-Verbal Communication?

Can we read everything just by looking at the eyes? Are the eyes the only signals we should concentrate on?

The thing is, the eyes are just one of the indicators or signals that we communicate with. When making high-stakes decisions duh as whether a person is guilty of a crime, pupil dilation is not something you solely rely on to make a judgment.

We should also look into context. That said, we are more perceptive to the body language of the people we always come into contact with compared to total strangers simply because we can tell their regular facial expressions apart from the non-regular ones.

To make better assessments of feelings, we need to look at various other evidence or elements of body language and course context. Because people cannot change how their pupils behave, the eyes are often used as a source of information to help create a better relationship simply because it enables us to empathize better. You may not be able to read a person's exact thoughts just by looking at their eyes but it still is a good perspective to study body language and read people.

CHAPTER 3
POSTURE AND ORIENTATION

The same way you train a dog to listen to your body language and cues, you can train a human being to follow you without question. The first step to control those around you lies in analyzing them, however, which is why this will discuss how to analyze people based on their body language.

Positive Body Language

There is a chance that you or someone you are observing is feeling insecure and trying to mask it. However, if you are not dealing with the melancholic personality, you might be dealing with a choleric personality. Everyone has heard the phrase "Fake it until you make it." This is the dogma of the choleric personality type. Whether they were cut out for something or not, they will not give up easily.

If you are confronting this type of personality, simply the mere act of uncrossing your arms or legs should gain you a little confidence. Add to that a genuine smile for the next person that you encounter and watch as they lighten up a bit in response. It might take a little practice, but this type of body language gives you control of the situation.

Understanding eye contact: This one can be tricky as it is easy to misinterpret but long eye contact is almost always meaningful in some way shape or form. If a person can look at you without looking away for more than a few seconds, then usually they are confident around you and are likely to be genuine. This is likely to be your phlegmatic personality type; one who is displaying a little bit of awkward shyness. They will notice you scanning the room, but do not count on them calling you out on this.

Typically, eye contact can make you look interested and says a lot about the person you are dealing with. If you find yourself being stared at by a person, you are likely dealing with a sanguine personality. This personality type is an observer and tends to be the sincerest of the four. By looking people in the eye, it is their way of proving those qualities.

Depending on the situation, you can look down and away out of shyness. When people are shy, they are deemed innocent. Your phlegmatic personalities are good at this as well. You want to seem innocent, no matter what your intentions as the best choice for drawing other people in are to keep them interested. Since you want people to trust you,

you have to get close enough to analyze what type of personality you are dealing with.

If the other party looks away and down, and then back up at you, take advantage of this opportunity to consider them more closely. This is a sign of vulnerability which means they trust you, so you are free to do with that trust what you may. This is often a good time to ask them about themselves or offer something personal to break the ice. Compliments are always a good choice as it is hard to dislike someone who has recently played you a compliment.

Smile: The most important asset anyone has is their smile. A smile is a window to the soul. If you are walking down the street and someone gives you a genuine smile, it can change your day. That is the power you want to carry around with you. This is the gift of most sanguine personality types. They are cheerful on the outside and can easily make people laugh. Faking a smile is hard. The truth of any smile lies in the eyes. Pay careful attention to the lines that form when the cheeks rise as the evidence of a genuine smile forms.

If you ask someone to do something and they decline, smile anyway, they will feel bad for saying no. Depending on their actual reaction, say it again in a different way and a cartoonish voice (humor), and follow up with a serious voice. Ask for the favor again by adding another smile. This is best used in social situations and is to be avoided at work. Unless you are super cool with your co-workers or if you are sure you are dealing with a sanguine personality.

If your co-worker or your boss display a dislike for emotions or seem impatient, you could be dealing with a choleric personality. You will need to make it seem like they are the leaders. You're pushing boundaries, but you don't want anyone to recognize this game. No matter how it ends, do not give too much of a reaction. If you are too happy, it could kill the vibe. The same is true if you are too upset, just smile. You will not be able to change your personality type as the theory is that you were born that way. However, knowing more about yourself, you can control the display, or even master your weaknesses to have influence or get close enough to other people, that you may sincerely analyze them.

Negative Personality Cues

Now that you have a basic understanding of positive body language, let us look at the opportunity to dig into the negative cues often given by different personality types. Sometimes even the most trustworthy and genuine people can give off signals of distress through body cues, so it is important to take them with a grain of salt to avoid being misled.

If you find someone who is trying to discourage you, or they are judging you, their personality is likely phlegmatic if the negativity you are picking up on is coming from someone who is demanding attention or seems phony; you are amidst a sanguine personality type. You want to know the difference and how to respond to either situation to achieve a goal. Whether it is to cheer someone up, so you can enjoy their company, or perhaps you need to get away from someone who would seek to destroy your aura. Either way, practice makes perfect, and observing takes a lot of it.

Personal space: If someone moves away from you, this is often a sign that they believe you either did something wrong or you represent something negative to them.

This mentality applies to all four of the personality types. It hurts to feel rejected. Instead of feeling sorry for yourself, move back into their realm if you want to change the vibe.

Body Language and Posture

Posture and general movement might also express a big deal of information. A study on body language has developed considerably since prehistoric days; however, well-known media have concentrated on the over-interpretation of protective postures, arm, and leg crossing. Whereas these nonverbal acts can show thoughts and attitudes, the study indicates that body language is far more restrained and less perfect than formerly believed.

Proxemics

Individuals often refer to the need for personal space which is as well a vital style of nonverbal communication. The level of space people needs and the level of space people tend to perceive as belonging to them are swayed by several factors comprising social models, intellectual potential, situational aspects, personality distinctiveness, and level of knowledge. For instance, the amount of individual space required when having an informal talk with another person frequently varies from one to four feet. On the contrary, the individual distance required when talking to a group of people is approximately eight to twelve feet.

Eye Gaze

The human eyes play an important role in nonverbal communication and such aspects as staring looking and blinking are considered significant nonverbal acts.

When people meet someone or things that they adore, the pace of blinking goes up and pupils enlarge. On the other hand, staring at another individual may show a variety of emotions comprising hostility, concern, and desirability.

People as well use eye gaze as a way to conclude if someone is being sincere. Usual, fixed eye contact is frequently taken as an indication that someone is telling the reality and is dependable. Deceitful eyes and failure to keep eye contact, on the contrary, is often perceived as a pointer that somebody is dishonest or being misleading.

Touch

Communicating by use of touch is another essential nonverbal conduct. There have been considerable amounts of study on the significance of touch in childhood and infancy. For instance, a baby raised by a negligent mother experiences lasting deficits in conduct and social relations. Touch generally might be used to communicate love, awareness, compassion, and other related emotions.

On the other hand, touch is similarly used as a technique to communicate both position and authority. Researchers have established that high-status persons tend to attack other people's individual space with superior rate and strength than lower-status persons. Gender differences as well play a part in how individuals use touch to bring out the intended meaning.

Appearance

People's preference for color, outfits, hairstyles, and other aspects affecting appearance is regarded as nonverbal communication. Research has confirmed that diverse colors might suggest different personal moods. Besides, appearance might also change physiological responses, judgments, and understanding. For instance, just imagine all the restrained decision people rapidly make about somebody based on their look. These initial impressions are vital, and that is why specialists propose that work seekers dress decently for interviews with likely employers.

Researchers have also established that appearance might play a part in how individuals are viewed and how much money they make. For example, a study carried out on attorneys established that attorneys perceived as more attractive than their workmates earned practically more than those viewed as less good-looking. Culture is a significant sway on how appearances are viewed. While slenderness is respected in Western cultures, some African cultures associate full-figured people with superior health, prosperity, and social class.

Artifacts

Items and images are as well as tools that might be deployed to communicate nonverbally. In an online discussion, for instance, people may pick avatars to symbolize their distinctiveness, and converse information on who they are, and the things they adore. People frequently spend time creating a particular picture and surrounding themselves with items planned to transmit information regarding the things that are vital to them. Uniforms, for instance, may be applied to share an amount of information regarding an individual. A warrior shall put on fatigues, a police force will dress in uniform, and a physician shall dress in a white lab coat. From a bigger perspective, a simple glance at this attire tells everybody what an individual does as an occupation

CHAPTER 4
NONVERBAL OF FEET AND LEGS

We naturally spend so much time observing all nonverbal communication above the waist that we often overlook the importance of the legs and feet in body language. Both have a lot to say, and, when combined with the other parts of the body, can be used expertly to understand and predict behavior.

How to Analyze People through Nonverbal Behaviors of the Legs

When analyzing the body language of the legs and feet, it is essential to recognize why internal feelings and thoughts manifest through them. Hand gestures are seen naturally as a communicative medium. It is because we write words with them, paint with them, clap or shoo away someone with them - they are inherently understood on a human level as being used for communication. We do not think about the legs and feet in the same way. They are for walking, kicking, and jumping - so why should we pay attention to them?

It is precisely because we overlook the legs and feet that we should pay attention to them. When trying to psychologically control our speech, hand gestures, trunk posture, facial expressions, and eye gestures, we put so many cognitive resources towards them that we forget ourselves about our legs and feet as ways to communicate. That makes them pretty unique. It means that our subconscious or true feelings are presented through them for the most part rather than deception.

That is a powerful thing to know when analyzing behavior. With that knowledge, you can decode a person's thoughts through how they use their legs and feet. To do so, pay attention to:

- Gait or stance

- Feet position

- Crossing or locking of legs and ankles

- Fidgeting feet and leg movement

Types of Leg and Feet Displays

There are several ways in which we display our legs and feet, subconsciously (and occasionally consciously) conveying our internal psychology through them. Some of the most important ones to look out for are:

Leg Crossing: Both men and women cross their legs. It can be similar to when the arms are crossed, protecting vulnerable parts of the body and being closed off. It is especially important when interpreting possible sexual thoughts. However, the most critical component is not the way the legs are crossed, but rather where they are pointing. When someone crosses their legs, but the legs or feet naturally point towards a person that conveys the opposite feeling - this is an open gesture, which means a person is willing to listen.

Ankle Crossing: When the feet cross over each other, and the arms are crossed, this "locking" posture is usually defensive. However, when the ankles are crossed, and the legs are splayed, this conveys a relaxed state.

Leg Splaying: Speaking of leg splaying, if crossed legs can imply a closed-off attitude when the legs are either parted widely (most commonly in men) or straightened out in a Y position when sitting, this conveys relaxation. However, it can also display a lack of care for how others perceive the person doing the leg splaying, which can imply recklessness. This takes up unnecessary space and can also be seen as an aggressive territorial claim.

Shaking or Wiggling: An extremely common stress adapter is leg shaking or feet wiggling. Many people are unaware they are even doing it. It implies anxiety of some kind, with the movements taking the mind away from those thoughts and calming the limbic system. It can also suggest irritation.

Foot Tapping: Subtly different from foot wiggling, the rhythmic tapping of the foot can, of course, simply mean someone is enjoying the pulse of the music. However, it can also mean that a person is feeling impatient and anxious to get moving.

Stride: Most feet and leg displays involve sitting down, but a pace while walking can tell us a lot about someone's state of mind. If the stride is stable and not overly hurried, then the person is feeling confident. If the pace is erratic and uncertain, then there is anxiety there, most probably some sort of social worry about how others perceive the walker.

Defensive Leg Displays: Keeping the knees clamped tightly together can be a dead giveaway that a person is feeling defensive. Of course, it can also be because a person is wearing a skirt, so always be mindful of how the context affects interpretation.

Hand Display and Leg Display Combinations

It is essential to be aware of specific hand displays that can be combined with leg displays, altering their meaning. It usually involves the touching of the legs in some way. When we talked about adapters, we mentioned hand cleansing, which is when a person rubs their hands on their thighs. It can alter how we perceive the leg position. For example, one ankle may be resting on the other thigh, creating an open, relaxed stance. However, when hand cleansing is introduced, this shows that there is some anxiety and that the leg position is only part of the picture. Likewise, someone could be sitting looking relaxed with their arms by their sides, but the legs are tightly crossed. Again, this gives us something to ponder. We must then look for other nonverbal cues that would allow us to weigh the two behaviors, giving us a better chance to figure out which one is most prevalent and current in the person's mind. Any self-touching of the legs can be interpreted as representing anxiety, even knee clasping when both hands are clasping one or both knees.

CHAPTER 5
NONVERBAL OF THE ARMS

Now that we understand the basics of where nonverbal communication comes from, its place alongside verbal communication, and how to analyze a person's body language, etc., we can now learn about specific gestures, postures, and expressions. These will help you predict and understand a person's thoughts and goals. How to Analyze People through Nonverbal Behavior of the Arms

The arms always depict some sort of nonverbal internal emotion or thought. It manifests as either a posture or a gesture. When analyzing the position of the arms, look for how the arms are held almost still. It could be in an open stance (arms extended out welcomingly) or a closed posture (arms folded defensively). When you analyze the gestures, look for how the arms move around.

Defensive Arm Displays

We have used the example of the arms folded in front of the body several times so far, and this is because it is one of the most common postures in nonverbal body language. It's also often one of the easiest to interpret. As we mentioned earlier, the arms are crossed in front of the stomach, which is a vulnerable area due to only being partially protected by the rib cage. It then is often seen as a protective stance. It is exhibited usually for one or more of the following reasons:

Feeling defensive at what is being accused or said. It could merely be disagreeing with the content of a significant other's speech.

Feeling nervous or anxious. By crossing the arms, not only is a person protecting themselves, but they are also trying to hide and not be noticed.

The person is feeling comfortable, and folding their arms is the most comfortable position for them to take at that time.

Notice how the last point disagrees with the first two. You must look for other nonverbal signs to either support or refute your initial interpretation. An example would be if the person were sitting down and locking their ankles together or crossing their feet. It is commonly seen with folded arms and is highly correlated with a defensive or negative attitude. Lastly, look for what the hands are doing alongside the folded arms. If they are clenched, this represents even more tension in the body and their attitude.

Arm Withdrawal

If you notice a person's arms being pulled inward towards their body, this can mean that they disagree with what you are saying, or even with who you are as a person. It can also convey disgust and anger. It can also represent apathy and a desire to withdraw from a conversation or situation. This movement can be significant, but it can also be subtle. Keep an eye out for anyone withdrawing their arms towards their body even slightly.

Arm withdrawal is often presented alongside leaning away from the speaker, facing away from them, or disgusted and bored postures and facial expressions. In some instances, the offending person does not even need to speak to cause this defensive behavior.

Arms Freeze Display

We naturally communicate with our arms and hands. These are among the most common gestures, and so movement in the arms is a continual way of communication. However, in some specific circumstances, these movements can halt. The arms become entirely still, often staying lifeless at the side of the body, but they can also freeze into other postures. This "Arm Freezing", is usually a sign that something is amiss. Remember earlier, we talked about the fight, flight, and freeze response? Arm freezing is the product of the freeze component. We tend to stay very still naturally when we believe there is a threat nearby. It is a way to avoid detection by dangerous human beings or animals. In this sense, then, arm freezing is usually a bad sign that a person doesn't just feel defensive, but that they feel threatened.

If someone presents this behavior, it could mean that they are overwhelmed with stress or that they feel ideologically or personally threatened by something or someone nearby. It is essential to recognize this behavior and try to set the person at ease if their arm freezing seems disproportionate.

The Self-Hug

How we have certain nonverbal behaviors which are designed to calm or vent a painful internal emotion? A self-hug is an excellent example of this. It can be seen when a person wraps their arms around the front of their body and then holds the outside of the opposite arm. There can sometimes be a rubbing or hugging motion as well. It is an adapter to make a person feel better if they are stressed. The stress can be slight or more pronounced.

We often naturally use this posture when preparing for a difficult situation like hearing bad news or waiting to face an exam. Caution should be taken; however, self-hugging can also mean a person is cold. Again, look for other nonverbal and verbal signs which will help you decide this behavior.

Territorial Arms Displays

The arms can be used to mark off territory. It can be a space or even a person. It is common to see partners with their arms around each other or arms locked together in public places. While this can be purely affectionate, it can also be a way to say to others, "this is my mate." Of course, we do not like to think of people as objects, but we have to remember how impulsive our brains can be. We are, after all, part ape, and those brain impulses are still competing alongside our humanity and even-mindedness. An example of this would be seeing your partner talking to someone attractive and then walking up and smiling while putting your arm around your partner. It is a definitive territorial behavior.

When marking off territory with the arms, you may also see people stretch out or lean against something with their arm or elbow. It is a way to say "this is mine." You might also see yawning used as an adapter in some situations, allowing a person to stretch their arms out around them. We accept that someone might stretch for comfort while yawning, but it is also often used to establish personal space. Moving the arms around, you can also mean that you want to be isolated and left alone.

Welcoming Arm Movements

We have focused heavily on adverse arm movements and postures, but the arms can also be used to say positive things. When arms are outstretched in front of a person, especially in a Y formation, this represents a hugging motion. Likewise, when a person opens up their body during conversation and the arms part to show their torso, this is a sign that they are responding to what is being said and welcoming of it. It can also be a sign of developing trust.

CHAPTER 6
NONVERBAL OF THE HANDS AND FINGERS

Hands and fingers are extensions of the arms but their association with communication is more commonly recognized by more people. A large part of this has to do with the fact that often we actively use our hands and fingers to communicate with other people. We use our hands and fingers to tell other people to stop or proceed, to encourage them or dissuade them, to signal peace or encourage confrontation, and a host of other gestures meant to say something.

The hands and fingers still send messages to other people when we are not aware. These are called passive nonverbal cues and they speak just as loudly as the passive gesture.

Both of these types of nonverbal uses depicted by the hands and fingers - active and passive nonverbal cues - are both important and we will explore the roles of these types of cues related to these parts of the body.

The hands and nonverbal communication

Hands and fingers play a huge role in the communication process. So much so that a whole system of communication has been developed around using them to communicate and this is called sign language. Sign language is the communication whereby a person uses hand and finger motions to substitute verbal communication. Sign language uses active hand and finger gestures. Active in this sense speaks to the fact that a person wants to communicate a certain message and therefore, deliberately uses a signal that sends this message.

Active hand gestures

Human beings did not start out using verbal communication as the primary way of expressing thoughts, feelings, and opinions. While the mouth was able to express grunts and other sounds, the range was not wide enough to allow our cavemen ancestors the ability to express all that they needed to survive. The hands were the saving grace in that time and thus, they were a communication tool among the many functions that they had and still have.

The use of the hands as a communication device has stuck with us through human evolution even though verbal communication has developed exponentially. Even verbal communication would not be as enriching as it is now without the use of the hands to enhance what is being said. Hands are the nonverbal complement to what is being verbally communicated and so, our brains have become hardwired through the evolution of our species to seek out what the hands have to say to complement what is being said or to contradict it. This is why we often pay so much attention to what the hands say. The brain is programmed to give the hands a great amount of attention when we read the messages someone else sends while we communicate, unlike the relative lack of attention it normally pays to feet and legs. The level of importance that we give to the hands when it comes to communication only comes second to the importance that we place on facial expression as a nonverbal communication device. The hands give solid hints as to what is happening to a person mentally and emotionally because more neural connections exist between the brain and hands compared to any other part of the body.

Not everyone is adept at interpreting the message that the hands send though even though we are hardwired to notice them during the communication process. Some people are better at reading hands compared to others. There is a scientific research that shows toddlers who use more hand gestures at that stage in their life have greater language abilities, and cognitive intelligence later on in their life.

The link between the hands and communication may be that not only is it relatively close to the brain, but also because the sense of touch grounds us to our parents and caretakers as babies. Touch is commonly done through the hands, and so we look for that touch from that moment.

The functions that the hands have when it comes to communication include:

- Substituting words. An example of this is holding up the hand to indicate that a person should stop rather than using the word itself.

- To support verbal communication with an illustration. For example, you can show a person how high you mean when you are talking about height by holding your hand up to the appropriate height.

- To give directions. A person may point to show where they are talking about even if they do not use cardinal points and direction-indicative words like north or south.

- To give a visual representation to support the verbal dialogue. For example, when talking about shape, you may use your hand to depict a circle or a square.

- To simplify complicated explanations. Sometimes the use of specific jargon or big words can make an explanation hard to understand but the use of gestures can support those items and make them simpler to understand.

Hand gestures and verbal communication go hand in hand so well that we most often move our hands in time to the message we are sending verbally.

Some hand gestures are easier to interpret in meaning compared to others and these are normally active gestures. Let's take a look at common active hand gestures now.

Hands are dangerous weapons

Before the invention of guns and even knives, humans had to defend themselves from different threats from other human beings, animals, plants, and more. Human beings had to defend themselves from these attacks and more, and therefore the most instinctive and ready weapons were hands.

There are a variety of ways that the hands can be used as weapons whether a person is on the offensive or defensive such as curling the fingers to form a fist, and pointing the fingers to form a shape resembling a spear.

Getting the point across that the hand can be used as a weapon does not mean that a person has to use it as such. Just forming a fist or other weapon look-alike can show another person that this person intends to or will use their hands in such a manner.

"I mean no harm"

As opposed to using the hands as a weapon, they can be used as a sign of peace and allegiance. This signal is done by opening the palms of the hand. The gesture can be done to show the other person that his person is not armed and is therefore not a threat. It is similar to a dog showing its throat to another as a gesture of submission or surrender.

Open palms are also linked to truth and honesty and this is why placing an open palm over the heart is done while making oaths in the courtroom. The gesture is performed by holding one or both palms open.

Opening the palm can also be a sign of apology or that a person did not mean to upset another.

Because this is a universal sign of truth, some people will deliberately use it as a way to deceive others. Therefore, you need to look out for contradicting body language if you ever suspect that person is lying to you while using this hand gesture.

Waving

This is a common active hand gesture that is often used as a greeting.

Despite the mostly positive connotation of this gesture, it can be negatively interpreted if not combined with positive body language. For example, if the wave is done with the back of the hand facing the other person, this can be seen as a dismissive gesture and thus, insult the other person.

Raised hands

Because the hands are such a powerful tool used in communication, a raised hand has been seen as a sign of authority or power over others for thousands of years. This gesture was so significant that all the people of power or authority had to do was simply raise their hand to signal that they had the floor and so, no one else was allowed to speak or interrupt during that time. This gesture dates back so far that persons of lower social status were executed for interrupting Julius Caesar in Roman history.

We live in a vastly different time and era now, but the raised hand still holds significance when used in social settings. Just look at the Italian and French cultures and you will notice that they are one of the societies that still place great significance on hand talking. In the Italian culture, taking a turn to talk in a group setting (even a group of just two) is a simple matter of raising your hand to signal that you want the floor. As a sign of respect to the talker, listeners will place their hands down or behind their back to show that they have recognized the symbol and are granting this person's request to hold the floor at that particular time.

The only trick is to get your hand up as fast as possible when you would like the floor to get a word in. Don't worry, this is not that difficult. It is a simple matter of looking away or touching another person's arm to show that you would like a turn to have the floor. The Italian culture is one where there is a lot of physical touch and outsiders might see this as being overly friendly and intimate but in actuality, Italians use such touching because they place great significance on these gestures to send messages in communication. They are smartly trying to restrict the gestures of each other's hands so that they can take the floor. They usually reserve the right hand for demanding that attention while articulating their points and showcasing their emotions with their left hand. Therefore, right-handed people have an upper hand in conversation in this culture. Pun intended!

Handshaking

This gesture is exhibited by people pressing their palms together and shaking their hands up and down an in-pumping action. This is typically a gesture of greeting but the meaning varies depending on how this gesture is performed. For example, the length of time that this is done suggests the meaning. Holding the handshake for too long - more than 3 pumps - can be seen as intimate, while doing it for too short a time normally raises suspicions.

How the palm feels also leaves an impression. For example, a wet palm during a handshake suggests that a person is sweaty because he or she is nervous.

The positioning of the handshake is also important. Shaking the hands evenly with palms facing the other person suggests that a person feels equally toward another. If a person twists the handshake so that their palm is over the other person's, suggests that they feel superior to the other person. Twisting the handshake so that the palm up suggests that a person feels submissive to the other person.

How tightly a person squeezes the other person's palm while shaking hands also makes an impression. Shaking the other person's hand too tightly is seen as a power play to assert dominance while a weak handshake suggests that this person is not only physically weak but also mentally and emotionally weak by comparison.

CHAPTER 7
NONVERBAL OF THE FACE

I f hand gestures are some of the fastest-changing nonverbal behaviors, then facial expressions are the most complex. Of course, facial expressions change over time, though not as quickly as hand gestures. What is most challenging about analyzing them is that they can be so nuanced. A small flicker of a look can appear for a moment - what did it mean? Was that an underlying thought bubbling to the surface? A momentary daydream? Facial expressions in their purest forms are simplistic, but it is how we, as human beings, mix possible combinations, which makes them so subtle at times.

How to Analyze People through the Nonverbal Behavior of the Face

Facial expressions can be proactive or reactive. It is through understanding this distinction that you will have a better success rate when analyzing key expression attributes. Dynamic facial expressions occur when they are "sent" out to be received. For example, if someone were to tell you a funny story and they start laughing and smiling as they are saying it - that's a proactive facial expression. It is intended to be received, and usually comes in tandem with a speech that is directed at another person. Do not mistake this for always being conscious of nonverbal communication. It is not. Sometimes a person chooses to smile while talking, but at other times the smile will come through subconsciously. What is essential here is to recognize that the facial expression is being broadcast as part of a message.

Reactive expressions happen when a person is receiving and responding to information. Taking the above example, although the person telling you the funny story is laughing, you start to frown. Why? Because you find the joke to be in poor taste. It again could be an instinctive reaction or one you deliberately broadcast, but what makes it reactive is that the facial expression is in response to something.

Think about these two broad categories of facial expressions as you analyze a person's behavior. Are they responding or sending? If they are sending out a facial expression while talking, then this is more likely to be what they want to be perceived. That does not mean it is accurate. If they are responding, then it is more likely that it is an instinctual response and, therefore, more representative of what is going on in their mind.

Of course, there are ifs, buts, and maybes surrounding these two categories. Sometimes a person can be sending out reactive expressions while talking because they are responding to their own emotions and how their communication is being received. In this way, all we can say about reactive and proactive expressions is that they tend to be presented when switching between receiving and sending messages.

What are Micro Expressions?

When we mentioned the nuance of facial expressions and how subtle they can be, we were referring to micro expressions. These are small movements of the face that reveal the true feelings and thoughts of a person. They are usually involuntary and great examples of emotional impulses from the limbic system pushing past an individual's defenses to being revealed to the outside world.

Facial expressions can be faked (more on that below). However, micro expressions are much more difficult to fake because of their involuntary nature. There are seven established micro-expressions, and each of them is connected to deep, visceral emotion. Be vigilant for each when analyzing someone.

These micro-expressions are:

Surprise: This manifests itself as having raised eyebrows, wrinkled brow, wide-open eyes, and often the jaw-dropping full and showing teeth. The surprise is relatively ambiguous as it can be either a negative response or a positive response.

Hate: Also referred to as contempt, it often presents itself with one side of the mouth raised. There can also be a furrowed brow, but hatred is often accompanied by a blank or apathetic expression.

Sadness: This emotion filters through onto the face with the lips curled down at the sides and a furrowed brow, which arches upward in the middle creating vertical and horizontal lines. The cheeks and muscles around the eyes can be tensed.

Happiness: When a moment of joy flickers across the face, it presents with no wrinkled brow, a smile, raised cheeks, and crow's feet at the sides of the eyes.

Disgust: This has a surprise component, though mixed with disgust. It manifests on the face with raised upper eyelids, curled upper lip with nose wrinkled, and the cheeks raised. It can also present with a furrowed brow, and the corners of the mouth curved downwards.

Anger: This presents itself with eyebrows lowering and furled in the middle. Often vertical lines appear between the eyebrows. Lower lids tense up and raise slightly. Pursed lips. Flaring nostrils. Gritting teeth. A focused stare, and also tilting of the head slightly downward, occasionally upward.

Fear: Perhaps the most instinctive emotion of all. It manifests as raised eyebrows that are curling towards each other in the middle of the brow—which causes the forehead to become wrinkled. As a surprise, the eyes are quite wide, but the lower lids do not pull down as much. The mouth will open with the chin, sometimes pulling in towards the chest.

Sometimes these micro-expressions can be present at the same time or in close proximately, so stay alert to such changes should they occur.

Facial Expressions can be faked!

We have mentioned the importance of deception in nonverbal communication. It is common practice for a deceptive individual to use facial expressions to fake communication or hide what they are thinking. However, as they are so intuitive, only the most seasoned (and sometimes sociopathic) can fake micro-expressions realistically.

That being said, it is essential to keep an eye out for common signs of deception. For example, someone who is smiling widely with their mouth, but their eyelids remain static, is most probably not that happy. Look for combinations of competing for micro expressions. If you see someone smile, but their brow is furrowed as if disgusted, you will see the conflict between what they are trying to show you and what they are thinking.

Isolated Nonverbal Expressions

As well as micro-expressions, there are several expressions and states which can be isolated to parts of the face. These can also help you to detect deception, but can also reinforce your interpretation of another nonverbal cue.

Stay aware of:

Eye Gestures: Just as the hands can make gestures conveying meaning, the eyes can too. Looking away and to the side, while talking, can mean deception as the person is trying to think through what they are saying, but it can also mean the person is trying to remember something. Too much eye contact seems unnatural, and again if someone is never breaking their stare, deception or an attempt at domination is likely. Staring at the ground or focusing on the hands can also be an adapter to alleviate nervousness. A glazed look shows disinterest or daydreaming. Even the dilation of the pupils can tell us something, with overly dilated eyes linked to forms of deception and arousal.

Glasses and Makeup: Remember that how the body interacts with the environment can contain vital clues about intent and desires. If a person wears glasses, for example, they can use these in a way which shows concentration (taking the glasses off and putting one of the arms in the mouth), or dislike (looking over the top of the glasses with the head tilted down). Makeup, which draws attention to the mouth and eyes are often misread as purely to attract a mate, but they are commonly used to portray confidence. In some circumstances, makeup can be an adapter of sorts to help reduce insecurity. The style of makeup used can also tell us how the individual feels about a specific situation in some circumstances (professional vs. personal).

The Lips: We have mentioned how the lips can convey the information above. They can smile when happy or relaxed, the corners can point down when sad or disgusted, and they can tense up or become pursed when stressed or worried.

Nose Flare Displays: Our nostrils flare to take in more air, and this often occurs when our pulse rate quickens. It can be due to anger or arousal.

Furrowed Forehead Display: The eyebrows convey much about how a person is feeling. What is fascinating about them is that with just a small alteration, they can appear to express an opposing emotion. When frowning, the eyebrows draw together, and this brings the forehead into play. When this happens in tandem, we can see annoyance, anger, or deep concentration.

Blushing and Blanching: Blushing has long been associated with feeling embarrassment or feeling attracted to someone. One theory behind the use of blush makeup is that it mimics this signal and therefore attracts people towards it. However, blushing can mean anxiety or a quickening pulse as the capillaries in the face open up. It can also be the case that a person has social worries about blushing, and this exacerbates the issue. It can also be a defensive reaction when deceiving someone. However, some individuals simply have a strong flush response, and that should not be read into much.

Smiles and Laughter: The World's Most Irresistible Gestures

Laughter and smiling are both powerful communicators. As you no doubt, realize by now, they are, like most nonverbal cues, capable of being presented consciously and subconsciously. What is so fascinating about the smile is that it is also the most common means of deception. The main reason it is used for is fraud because people are naturally treated more positively when they smile, in some cases, even receiving more lenient sentences in the courts. It is called the smile leniency effect, and it is why lying through smiling is so commonly attempted.

It is not always easy to spot, but fake smiles can be identified by:

A Lack of Closed Eyes: Smiling brings about changes in the upper face. This includes the eyelids narrowing. If the eyes are wide or cold looking, then the smile is only skin deep.

No Crow's Feet: The orbicularis oculi muscle creates wrinkles around the eyes when we smile. However, when someone is faking a smile, this muscle often does not engage.

Showing Lower Teeth: When someone fakes a smile, they sometimes show their lower teeth. When we smile naturally, the cheekbone major muscle group pulls the smile upward, which means the bottom teeth should fully or partially obscure the lips. If you can see a lot of the lower teeth, this may suggest deception.

Smiles come in many shapes and sizes, but psychologists have identified five main types. By being able to differentiate between them, it is possible to become a far more skillful reader of facial expressions.

The five smile types are:

1. The Seductive Smile: This smile is used to either gain favor or signal attraction. It involves a subtle smile but with extended direct eye contact and then a slow glancing away. It also includes submissive head tilting to the side or downward.

2. Sarcastic Smile: Here, the mouth is upturned as though happy. Sometimes the mouth is a crooked smirk, and there is always a look of mocking disbelief or disdain in the eyes.

3. Fake Smile: We've covered this one extensively.

4. Uncomfortable Smile: This smile is usually born out of nervousness. It is often a way to satisfy someone who has said something you do not agree with, but you do not want to get into a confrontation about it. The smile is often closed-lipped, and the eyebrows raise slightly and curl up in the center.

5. Duchenne Smile: Coined by psychologist Paul Ekman, this smile is the real deal - it expresses real happiness. It is the polar opposite of a fake laugh complete with narrowing eyelids, crow's feet, with the cheeks raised.

CHAPTER 8
HOW TO SPOT EMOTION WITH BODY LANGUAGE

Reading and analyzing people is a skill. Like most skills, some people master them easily while others have to learn. Think about it like coding. Some children master coding skills at an early age, and by the time they hit their teenage years, they are very good at coding and can hack some of the most secure systems. On the other hand, some people learn to code later on in life. They get through life oblivious of their potential in computer science, but when they start learning, they become masters. This is what happens with reading people.

It does not matter when you learn to read people. What matters is how good you are at it and what you do to improve your skills. To be honest, this is an important skill that you will be well suited to learn. It can save you in many situations. You might not be able to read someone's mind, but you can read what you see in their actions and what you hear in their words. That counts for something because you have tangible evidence upon which you base your actions.

In as much as you will learn how to read people, you must also be aware of your weaknesses. Even some of the best analysts out there will, from time to time, struggle to set aside their experiences, unconscious bias, or normal influence and knowledge of human nature.

Before you claim awareness of what someone is thinking, you have to step back and question the basis of your knowledge. Do you have information or evidence to back your analysis? Are you sure you are not projecting your personal experience on the subject to conclude? Of all the information you have about the subject, do you believe you have thoroughly analyzed them all before making a decision? More importantly, is the information in your possession credible and thorough enough to rule out any other possibility behind the subject's behavior? If you can do that, you will have an honest and accurate analysis of the subject.

In many cases, when you believe you have a hunch about someone, it is no more than your personal bias clouding your judgment. From there, you can make an incorrect decision about them, yet deep down, you believe you are correct. Critical thinking must be an important part of such assessments. The ability to read people is a skill, an important one that we should all learn.

It is easier to read some people than others. In a powerful position, it is wise to make the participants feel comfortable. Relax the situation so that they feel comfortable enough to express themselves freely. This way, you have a better chance of analyzing their feelings and thoughts clearer.

How many times have you come across poker face in conversations? People throw it around randomly even when it's not necessary, but it alludes to someone who can conceal their emotions and feelings by keeping a straight face. Such a person can be sad but interact jovially with everyone, masking their deep pain. Many reports suggest that spoken words only account for 7% of communication. Further, they suggest that body language and tonal variation account for 55% and 38% respectively (Wiesenthal, Silbersweig, and Stern, 2016).

While the population samples for these studies might vary from each situation, the concept is true. Therapists and clinical psychologists read so much into their patients' lives by observing their facial expressions and body language while in session. Many patients are defensive and only come to therapy because they are made to. To get out of therapy, they spin tales of how they are doing well already and feeling better and can reintegrate into society. However, the therapist is trained to notice the disconnect between their actions and words.

The therapist will try to find an action pattern at different parts of the conversation, most of them unrelated, and use this to assess whether the patient is honest about their words or not. It is not just about telling whether the patient is healed or not; it is also about helping them heal. A lot of people also come to therapy as a last resort. Everything else has failed them, and they need to find solace in someone or something. By understanding body language, therapists can genuinely show empathy and encourage the patient to stay strong.

This is another technique of creating a healthy environment where the patient can knock down their boundaries and allow the therapist to understand their pain and distress and eventually help them overcome their tribulations.

Let's take another example—parenting. Many parents have a deep (if not intimate) understanding of their children. Despite the brave face that your child might show, you know something is not right. You can feel the depression. You know a certain behavior pattern in your child, and when that pattern changes abruptly, you are wise to know something is amiss.

Many children struggle in life, especially as they approach their teen years. They struggle because they feel no one understands them. This is how they end up finding help in the wrong places because someone was keener on their behavior than the people closest to them. Such people eventually exploit their innocence.

To be fair to parents, understanding and reading teenagers is not easy. They are at a point in their lives where hormonal changes and interaction with the rest of the world conflict with everything that they might have learned about life growing up. It is so confusing for them. Most of them embrace their true identity at this point, and it might be different from what you might have expected of them growing up. As the development advances, their ability to conceal their real feelings also grows, especially if they feel they are going in a different direction than what you expect of them.

CHAPTER 9
HOW TO SPOT A LIE WITH BODY LANGUAGE

The Psychology of Lying

Lies. They have so much more power than we give them credit for. Lies have been responsible for causing trouble, damaging relationships, destroying trust and reputation. Lying involves two parties - the one who is deceiving, and the one who is being deceived. The deceiver, in this case, purposefully communicates the wrong information and gives false impressions deliberately. Throughout our lives, everyone is going to be playing the role of deceiver at some point, and other times, we could be playing the role of the one who is being deceived.

Why are we so quick to believe someone's lies at times? Are we just plain gullible? Or do we feel so overwhelmed cognitively that it is simply easier to believe what someone is telling us, rather than search for the truth? University of Virginia's psychologist, Bella DePaulo (Ph.D.) conducted a study and found that lying was in fact, a condition of life. DePaulo's study revealed that most people lied at least once or twice a day. It is as common as brushing your teeth or drinking water. Both men and women did it, and there were some relationships, such as that between a parent and a teenager, in which deception was higher than ever.

We know lying is wrong, yet why do we do it? We use the terms "little white lie" to sometimes even justify our actions and ease our conscience. The simple truth of the matter is, people, lie because they cannot help themselves. It has become almost second nature to us to try and hide the truth when we feel there is a need for it. We use it to bail us out of awkward situations, we use it to strengthen relationships which we know are going to benefit us at some point, we lie to be kind and to spare someone's feelings, we lie to enhance our social standing, and we lie to keep us out of trouble. Lying has become something of a survival mechanism, and that is why humans will always be prone to telling a lie.

Signs Someone Is Lying

Our bodies tend to give us away. There are telltale signs which indicate when someone might be less than honest. Nobody likes being caught in a lie or being told they are a liar. When the lie comes from someone you know, love, or trust, that painful trust can be even more disappointing.

When you get caught lying in a professional setting, that will completely jeopardize your reputation and kill any chance of having a career.

Some scenarios where a person could lie - or be required to lie - include the following:

• When It's Habitual - A classic scenario of when someone may habitually lie is when they say "I'm fine" even when they are not. Sometimes, this is done out of courtesy because they don't want to burden someone else with their problems. Other times, it could be because they're so used to saying they're fine that it's on autopilot now and they don't even think about it anymore. They may even lie if they don't want to encourage more questions because they don't feel like talking about it or involving someone else in their problems. Everyone has done this at least several times in their life, where they lie about being fine when they are not.

• As A Form of Deflection - Politicians are especially apt at this one, as they rely on extensive use of body language and verbal lies to deflect questions which they don't want to answer. In this scenario, they attempt to deflect you from paying attention to what matters through this form of distraction.

• When It Is Expected - In a legal setting is where you would see this happening most often, hence the term plausible deniability. This form of lying is expected, perhaps even customary as part of the job. Certain scenarios such as adhering to nondisclosure agreements and cross-company relationships are an expected part of some jobs. Then some jobs require you to think fast on your feet and respond while simultaneously protecting information. In these scenarios, lying is expected of you. Some people also may feel the need to lie because they don't like revealing their weaknesses to others, and they may try to cover that negative trait by lying and turning it into something positive instead.

Are They Telling Me the Truth?

How do you spot when someone is potentially telling you a lie? Especially when lying can take on so many forms during the day. The answer? By analyzing them and paying exceptional attention to spot when someone is being dishonest with you. When it comes to analyzing people to potentially spot dishonesty, here's what you need to keep in mind:

Observe When They Attempt to Deny: One of the most important things you need to listen to is the direct denial of an accusation. They will attempt to justify or defend themselves instead of directly addressing the question posed to them. They might respite to giving answers such as not likely, not exactly, not for the most part are common examples of what someone might say when they're attempting to deny an accusation. The next time you observe someone not giving you a definitive answer, they might very well be lying for some reason.

Avoid Speculating: Analyzing and speculating are two different things. When someone crosses their arms, we shouldn't just speculate that they are being closed off or annoyed without analyzing all the facts which are presented in front of us. Crossing the arms in front of the chest is a classic example of a body language gesture which often gets misunderstood because it could hold so many meanings to it. What you should do instead is to analyze the other elements which led to this move. Did this person cross their arms in response to a question? The first sign of deceptive behavior that happens in the first five seconds of the question asked will enable you to determine if that question was the one that produced the folded arms. This first clue of deception could even happen while the first question is being asked, which goes to know that this person's brain is moving much faster than the words coming out of the interviewer - it is a sign that they are subconsciously trying to frame their response. Keep an eye out for clusters of behavior, too, and whether this is a direct response to a question.

Avoid Being Biased: Remember the story of the boy who cried wolf? The little boy was dishonest several times until one day, he was finally telling the truth but nobody believed in him anymore. This story goes to show that even dishonest people are capable of telling truths now and then. To analyze if someone is being dishonest in a situation requires you to focus on the truthful responses they give while filtering out all the other information. Certain individuals are capable of telling truths while simultaneously lying at certain points in their story, and by keeping an eye on the essential information, you avoid being distracted by the untruths in their tale.

Observing When They're Being Evasive: Those who tell tall tales often include a lot of unnecessary fluff and long explanations in their stories, all the while never really addressing the issue at hand. Beating around the bush is how you would best sum it up. Redirecting and deflecting their responses is something they have become adept at doing, and they will try to distract you by even sometimes turning your question into another question. Have I ever done this before? Don't you know me well enough to know that I wouldn't? Don't I have a good reputation? These are just some of the many examples and ways in which someone might act evasively. If you observe that someone is doing this for a good 15 minutes or more and blatantly avoids directly answering your questions, it could be a good indicator that they are trying not to get caught in a lie.

Be On the Lookout for Signs of Aggression: If someone is quick to anger and becomes defensive when asked a question, that raises a red flag that there may be something going on, more than what they are willing to let on. When an individual begins to get defensive, angry, perhaps even aggressive, they may attempt to turn things around and make it seem like you are the one who is in the wrong. They could accuse you of being biased, discriminatory, and more, making it appear as though it was your fault. The blame game is a common technique used by those who are being dishonest.

Observe Their Body Language: And of course, there is the ever-faithful, natural lie detector that never fails - body language. A person's words could tell the most convincing, believable story you've ever heard, but their body will give them away before their minds can catch up. A subtle facial gesture is all it takes to give the game away, and if you're keenly observing them, these clues will be hard to miss. A person could touch their face or nose or even cover their mouth or face because this is another subconscious way of hiding a lie. The stress of deception can also cause the skin to turn cold and start itching or even flush - notice when they suddenly scratch their ears or nose. Look out for anchor point movements such as the changes in the arms or even the feet. Has the person suddenly started tapping their feet nervously? Or sweating profusely?

All of these situations are important to watch and you must also watch the cluster of behaviors and activity as opposed to zoning in on only one behavior. Spotting whether someone is telling a lie or the truth can be hard at first. It certainly requires training to efficiently tell if someone is lying so don't be disheartened because you're not able to do it right away. It is almost impossible.

Studying the Body Language of Liars

Perceiving a falsehood when you hear one can be a generally excellent ability to have throughout everyday life. Perhaps you are tired of finding past the point of no return that somebody has deceived you. Or on the other hand, maybe you are famously guileless and simple to trick. And when you are tired of being deceived, you can build your capacity to perceive a lie with an iota of exertion on your part.

Search for pressed together lips. At the point when an individual lies, their mouth generally winds up dry in the meantime because of the uneasiness and anxiety from lying. Because of this, the liar may press together their lips or make a sucking motion. If you see white on their lips, it's a marker that they are pressing together their lips and might lie.

Notice and when they shield their eyes or mouth. Our cerebrums subliminally give away little intimations through our conduct when we lie. For instance, it is regular for individuals to cover their mouths when they lie or to conceal their eyes from the individual they are lying to.

•If an individual puts their hands to cover their mouth, this can be a marker of a falsehood.

•The most basic way that somebody shields their eyes is by shutting them. This does exclude ordinary squinting – however delayed eye shutting checks.

Watch for anxious squirming. Liars frequently have a spike in tension dimensions since they are apprehensive about concealing the reality and afraid of being caught. The body wants to disperse this tension and it frequently shows in apprehensive squirming of some sort which is a signal to get the hidden emotions on the person's face.

•This can incorporate preparing signals like hauling your hair behind your ear, altering your tie, or rectifying your skirt. These changing positions give an analysis of people's intentions and you should always take note of these changes as they reveal things subconsciously.

•It can likewise incorporate hand to face movements like pulling on your ear or modifying the position of your glasses.

•Additionally, this may show as face language and it reveals more emotions on the outer part of the body. This includes repositioning your telephone or moving a glass of water when conversing with someone.

Watch the movement of their eyes. At the point when individuals are lying, the cerebrum frequently gives little markers through the eyes because the individual is awkward or on edge about saying the truth. Watch for fast squinting or eyes dashing forward and backward as indications of lying.

•Eyes shooting forward and backward show that an individual feels caught and they are searching for an exit plan – this could be both physically (they need to escape the room and make tracks in an opposite direction from the circumstance making them lie) and inwardly (they need to escape coming clean).

•When someone blinks at regular intervals, you should understand what that is passing across. And when somebody blinks more often in a conversation, it could be a marker that they are lying – particularly and when they squint 5 or multiple times quickly in succession.

The art of recognizing sudden changes in Tone and voice

Consider how they speak normally. When you notice an individual more often than not talks gradually and talking in all respects rapidly and confusing their words, it's most likely a sign that they are lying. Watch for changes in verbal conduct as an indication of lying. So, you should always take note of people's words and how they pitch the same, this allows you to know their point of view and what they mean.

•If you are attempting to decide whether an individual is lying and you don't have any acquaintance with them as of then, just pose them a few questions to inquire what you know the response to (like their name or calling. This is to measure how they talk regularly and at that point get some information about the thing you figure they may lie about.

•An individual's typical conduct in low-stress conditions is called their "benchmark." and this shows how the person could control himself. When you notice an inconsistent move in their communication baseline, then you should sense a foul play.

Watch out for people who love distancing themselves. Individuals who lie regularly always find pleasure in attempting to remove themselves from the falsehood. This implies they regularly avoid utilizing individual pronouns about themselves like "I," "me," or "mine." Sometimes they employ the use of these words in the typical discourse, yet watch out for diminished utilization contrasted with how they ordinarily speak.

•Liars may likewise utilize "him" and "her" rather than individuals' names more often in a communication channel and you should take note of this tip when trying to analyze if someone is saying the truth or not.

Look for long-winded responses. Sometimes people who lie give indirect, long-winded responses to straight-forward questions that could have received a simple answer. Rambling is a sign of nervousness that often occurs when someone is lying.

Of course, you should consider the person's normal manner of speaking. Some people just ramble when they speak normally. So, keep this in mind.

Watch their manner when speaking. The liar will seem nervous, speak quite quickly, and want to change the subject or leave as soon as they can. They may get defensive if you repeatedly ask them probing questions such as "Are you sure?" and "Is that the complete truth?" because they want to deflect attention away from the lie.

What to do to make lies obvious

As far as I can tell, individuals who pose this extremely summed up an inquiry, dependably have quite certain worries as a primary concern.

Noting all these in a manner helpful to you will necessitate that you uncover more in the method for particulars.

For instance, the motivation behind why a given explicit individual tells a ton of falsehoods can be anything from obsessive causes (dysfunctional behavior) and commitment to winning through double-dealing.

Yet, and when you are attempting to make sense of why we go over varieties of individuals who lie in a general manner, the reasons will be extraordinary. For instance, some basic human collaborations are socially planned around individuals misleading one another, more often than not in generally innocuous ways.

In early social communications, loads of more youthful individuals will in general untruth since they learn (kind of coincidentally) as little youngsters, that getting anything they need that grown-ups don't need them to have (which would incorporate sex), is most effectively increased through falsehoods. They frequently believe that lying is a flat out need.

Pose testing inquiries. The more inquiries you pose to them, particularly questions requiring profundity and detail, the more awkward they will move toward becoming because they should make up to an ever-increasing extent. They may repudiate themselves or lead themselves into a trap.

•It is extremely difficult to totally create a nitty-gritty story on the spot so search for chinks in their defensive layer. And when you truly give them an exhaustive round of questioning they may even in the long run disintegrate and concede they are lying (however don't depend too vigorously on this occurrence).

•Ask them a few times to clarify the succession of occasions. This is difficult to keep straight for somebody who is lying and it is likely they will commit an error.

•Ask them little insights regarding the thing they're lying about – like what shading their shirt was or how they felt when they saw somebody.

Consider past direct and offenses. In case the individual you consider lying has lied already, they will undoubtedly lie now. Think about how the individual would ordinarily act in this condition and balance it with their theorized lie.

•For precedent, and when you are an educator and you think your understudy is lying concerning why they haven't gotten their work done once more, contrast their reason with past reasons to check whether they constantly will, in general, be detailed, outlandish, or identified with a specific reason.

Ask the liar for any kind of help. In case you're experiencing difficulty making sense of something, a legitimate individual will enable you to conceptualize to concoct an answer. A liar won't have any desire to give you a larger number of subtleties or data than they are required to.

•Try posing inquiries like, "Would you be able to consider any other person who may have approached this PC?" If the individual attempts to enable you to make sense of another probability, they are most likely coming clean. Yet, and when they state they have no clue or respond adversely/forcefully, they are likely lying.

When the Face Gives the Game Away

Our faces are one of the most revealing, honest parts of our bodies. Without saying a word, your face can convey every emotion with such depth that people will be able to tell what you're feeling if it is expressed strongly. Crying, laughing, frowning, stress, anxious, depressed, nervous, all of these emotions flash across our faces when we feel them within us. Sometimes, even though we may want to cover up our feelings, our bodies don't necessarily cooperate, and our expressions become apparent on our faces for anyone observant to notice.

It is the signals in our body that will reveal the truth at the end of the day. Most of the time, we are completely unaware that our face is giving the game away. We may think we're doing a good job of covering up our emotions and putting on a mask, but without even realizing it, a slight slip of the mask is all it takes for the truth to snake its way out.

The reason why our faces are incapable of hiding the truth is because of the conflicting emotions that are happening within us. Whenever we're occupied with trying to tell a lie, certain thoughts may be going through our minds simultaneously. It is these thoughts that are shown for a split second across our faces. This is what gives us away. This split-second emotion is what reveals the way that we truly feel.

Why is it so difficult to tell a lie? Because our subconscious mind knows what's truly going on and it is acting independently from the verbal lie that we are telling everyone else. This is why our body language becomes out of sync with the words we are saying because our mind is not working in sync. Those who rarely tell a lie are the ones who are most easily caught. Since they haven't had much practice, their bodies don't know how to respond fast enough to the contradictory lie that they are telling, which makes their body language signals even more obvious than ever. They may believe that they have been convincing, but their bodies are telling a completely different story through a nervous gesture or a facial twitch which accompanies the lie.

Certain people have mastered the art of lying so well that they are much harder to spot. People like lawyers, politicians, actors, TV personalities, and even professional liars, for example, have perfected their technique and refined their body language gestures to a point where their lies become a lot harder to spot. People believe these individuals a lot more easily because the lies are harder to see. How did they accomplish this seemingly miraculous feat of being able to trick the body into not revealing a lie? They spend time practicing. They practice what they think feels like the right gestures when they tell a lie, and this long-term practice has been done over a long time. They have also practice minimizing their gestures, forcing themselves to keep their bodies calm and neutral when they're lying. It isn't easy, but it is certainly doable through lots and lots of practice.

Spotting a Lie - The Most Common Gestures Used

Certain gestures are used more than others during a lie. When you learn how to recognize them, that's when you start recognizing all the other cues to look out for which the lying individual may be displaying. Here are some of the most commonly used gestures during a lie, so the next time you suspect someone may be untruthful to you, see if you can spot the following telltale signs:

Covering the Mouth – Subconsciously, our brain is trying to tell us to stop the lies that are coming out of our mouths. Our bodies know what we're saying isn't true, and the mind is trying to prevent or resist the act of lying, which is why some people inadvertently put their hands across their mouths. An act of trying to "cover up a lie". This gesture can sometimes manifest in the form of someone trying to fit their fist into their mouth, too. Some people even try to cover up this gesture by pretending to cough. Actors often assume this gesture when they are playing the parts of criminals in movies or TV shows. When the "criminal" gets caught, the actors subtly incorporate this gesture into their acting like their way of cueing the audience in that they are being deceitful and dishonest. If someone uses this gesture when they are speaking, it could be indicative of a lie. If someone exhibits this gesture when you are speaking, it could be that they feel you are hiding something. We even see this gesture being exhibited in children at times, through the innocuous "shhh" where one finger is placed over the lips to indicate a secret. The next time you notice this gesture in someone, keep an eye out because something may be amiss in their story.

Nose Touch - Some people may rub their noses quickly. Some may just rub their nose in one, quick motion which may be almost imperceptible. Whether this indicates some-one is fibbing or not would depend on the context. Sometimes, they could be feeling unwell, or their nose could be itchy when certain elements are present. Research con-ducted by the Smell and Taste Treatment and Research Foundation revealed that when a person lies, a particular chemical which is known as catecholamines gets released. This chemical is then responsible for the swelling of the nose, especially during intentional lying. This is also the chemical that causes someone's blood pressure to increase. When our noses swell thanks to the blood pressure, we're left with a "tingling" sensation which results in an itch in the nose, which explains why some people briskly rub their noses when they're lying. Almost as though they were trying to scratch an itch. Analyzing Bill Clinton's testimony on his affair with Monica Lewinsky, it is noticeable that Clinton rarely ever touched his nose when he was lying. However, when he did lie, there would be a slight frown that lasted only for a split second, followed by a quick nose touch. How do you distinguish between when someone is lying and when they just have an itchy nose? Well, when someone is generally experiencing a nose itch, they will deliber-ately scratch or rub their nose, whereas those who use the lying gesture involves light strokes to the nose.

Eye Rub - The rubbing of the eyes is our subconscious brain's way of trying to block out what we perceive to be deceitful or distasteful. Men tend to do this more so than women, who will usually exhibit this move in the form of gentle touch motions just below the eye area. Some people exhibit the eye rub maneuver when they want to avoid looking at a person directly in the eye because they know they are lying to them.

Ear Grab - Have you ever spotted someone tugging at their earlobe when they answer a question? This gesture is sometimes associated with the act of lying, but at other times, it could be indicative of other things. This gesture is also exhibited by a person who is experiencing anxiety. Again, this move would depend on the context in which it is exhibited. In Italy, for example, the ear grab means something different entirely and is used to signal when someone is effeminate or gay.

Neck Scratch - This often accompanies the ear-grabbing signal. A person who is lying could exhibit this move by scratching the side of their neck just below the earlobe (if they don't do the earlobe move). This gesture is not only used when someone is telling a lie but also gets displayed when they are feeling doubtful or unsure about something. It can be a very telling sign if it is accompanied by verbal cues that contradict this gesture. For instance, if a person says yes, I can understand where you're coming from but ac-companies it with a neck scratch, this could be an indicator that they do not understand at all, and they are just agreeing with you for the sake of doing so.

CHAPTER 10
BEHAVIOR ANALYSIS

When Talking About Behavior Analysis, we focus on using learning principles to bring behavioral change. This is a branch of psychology that aims to understand the unforeseen cognitions and focuses on the behavior of a person and not on the mental causes of said behavior.

Behavior analysis has extremely fruitful practical applications when it comes to mental clarity and health, especially in helping children and adults learn a new sense of behaviors or reduce certain problematic behaviors.

Analyzing Social Behaviors

The intentions behind certain actions of ours are commonly hidden. When a person is feeling angry or feeling depressed for example, their behavior portraying this feeling is usually very different such as they would keep quiet or go for a smoke to calm down.

Another example is also the kind of words used to convey dissatisfaction such as 'sure, go ahead' or 'fine' when we are not fine with the solution or the decision made. Empathy is much-needed when it comes to analyzing social behaviors such as this because, at the end of the day, you want to understand and listen and not just hear to answer.

In analyzing behaviors, demonstrating trust, and building rapport are extremely crucial because when you display empathy, you naturally break down any subversions and focus on the heart of the matter.

A rule to remember is that when you do experience emotions and feelings, you must know that people around you will not know about it unless they sense a change in your body language. When nobody understands or gets it, there is no need to get angry—but of course, it is easier said than done. We get angry when nobody, especially someone close to us doesn't notice that we are angry.

Behavior Is Largely Dictated By Selfish Altruism.

Nobody is completely selfish and if we were to make such a claim, that would mean we are ignoring the acts of sacrifice, kindness, and love that go around the world. However, most behavior does come out from the elements of selfish altruism.

It is a win/win situation when it comes to selfish altruism. It is a basic two-way road of you help me, I will help you. Here are a few scenarios where selfish altruism applies:

1. Transactions: If you were to purchase a car, both the seller and the buyer mutually benefit. The buyer gets the vehicle; the seller gets their sales. This is a primary form of selfish altruism between two people who do not have any kind of emotional bond.

2. Familial: Our mind is designed to protect the people with whom we share our genes. We have a higher tendency to protect these people and this sense of protectiveness depends on close friends to loved ones to siblings and family.

3.   Status: People sometimes, not all the time, help someone as a sign of power. Sometimes, people offer assistance and help to boost their reputation and self-esteem.

4. Implied Reciprocity: Plenty of relationships are based on the fact that if I assist you one day, you would remember it and help me out as well one day when I need it.

Some certain behaviors are not part of the categories described above. For example, nameless heroes dying for a cause that does not directly benefit their country or blood-line. Another example is volunteers who devote their time selflessly towards missions and aids. But of course, these are just the smaller portion of the entire world community. The motives of people and what appeals to them is what you need to understand. When you do, you find ways to help people within these four categories. It's very rare not to expect people to give aid that does not benefit them in any form or way.

People Have Poor Memories.

Not everyone has a bad memory, but our minds have both long-term memory storage and short-term memory storage. For example, ever been introduced to someone at a party and then you just forgot their name the day after? People have trouble remembering things, especially something not relevant to be stored in their long-term memory. People are more likely to remember similarities that they share with you rather than differences.

When analyzing people, remember that people generally forget things so do not assume that they are disinterested with the information you have given or have malice against you.

People Are Emotional.

People have stronger feelings about certain things more than they let on but they can't show their specific emotions too much, especially negative emotions such as anger, outbursts, and depression simply because it is generally frowned upon by society. The rule is not to assume everything is fine just because someone isn't having an outburst. Sometimes the strongest ones are the ones that suffer most. All of us have some form of a problem, and these issues are normally contained. You necessarily do not need to call people out on their private deception, but what you need to do is be a little sensitive to those unseen currents and empathize with people because this gives you an advantage when you are trying to help.

People Are Lonely.

When you look at all these Instagram influencers having the time of their life or even celebrities going to numerous parties and ceremonies, the last thing you'd think is that they are lonely. The reality is, many people who seem like they have it all are quite lonely. People are sensitive to threats of being left out or ostracized or even having the fear of missing out. Loneliness and the desire to be among people exist in all of us, even if we are introverts. Analyzing this behavior is knowing that loneliness is very common among people and in this sense, you're not alone in feeling this way.

People Are Self-Absorbed.

Like it or not, people tend to be more concerned about themselves than about other people. Just look at social media and you can see how self-absorbed people are especially with an account full of selfies. People are more concerned more about themselves to give you any attention and for people to be lonelier, more emotional, and feel different than they let on depends also on how you see the world. This perspective makes you independent and also proactive at the same time when you think about it. You become independent so you do not have to rely on anyone and you are more proactive so you have things to do and places to go on your own without depending on enjoying good times with other people. You place your happiness in your hand rather than in the hands of other people.

When analyzing people, just remember that in some ways or another, they all think and act like you in varying degrees.

CHAPTER 11
COMMON PATTERNS OF INTERPRETING BEHAVIOR

Human behavior is a complex thing. Because of its complexity, reading and analyzing people is not as easy as it sounds—but neither is it hard simply because as human beings, we exhibit more or less the same kinds of mannerisms and behavior when we experience a certain emotion or action.

So What Exactly Is Behavior?

Essentially, scientists categorize human behavior into three components:

- Actions

- Cognition

- Emotions

Actions Are Behavior.

An action is regarded as everything that constitutes movement and observation whether using your eyes or using physiological sensors. Think of actions as a form of transition or even an initiation from one situation to another. When it comes to behavioral actions, these can take place at different scales and they range from sweat gland activity, sleep, or food consumption.

Cognitions Are Behavior.

Cognitions are described as mental images that are imprinted in our minds and these images are both nonverbal and verbal. Verbal cognitions are such as thinking 'Wow, I wonder what it's like to wear a $2000-dollar designer dress' or 'I have to get the groceries done later' all constitute verbal cognition. However, imagining things, in contrast, is considered nonverbal cognition, such as how your body will look after losing weight or how your house will be after a repaint. Cognition is a combination of knowledge and skills and knowing how to skillfully use them without hurting yourself.

Emotions Are Behavior.

Emotion is any brief conscious experience that is categorized by intense mental activity and this feeling is not categorized as coming from either knowledge or reasoning. This emotion commonly occurs or exists on a scale starting with positive vibes such as pleasurable to negative vibes such as being unpleasant. Other elements of physiology indicate emotional processing—such as an increase in respiration rate, retina dilation, and even increase in heart rat—all a result of increased or heightened arousal. These elements are usually invisible to the naked eye. Emotions, similar to cognitions also cannot be noticeable to the naked eye. These can only be noticed through tracking facial electromyography activity (FEMG) indirectly which monitors the arousal using ECG, analyzes facial expressions, respiration sensors, galvanic skin response as well as other self-reported measures.

Everything Is Connected

Cognitions, emotions, and actions run together and simultaneously with one another. This excellent synergy enables us to understand the events, activities, and happenings that are happening around us, to get in touch with our internal beliefs and desires, and to correctly or appropriately respond to people that are in this scenario.

It is not that easy to understand and determine what exactly is the effect and cause. For example, when you turn your head, which is an action, and seeing a face familiar to you, this will cause a burst of joy, which is the emotion and is usually accompanied by the realization which is the cognition. In other words, it is through this equation:

ACTION = EMOTION (joy) + cognition (realization)

In some other scenarios, this chain of effect and cause can also be reversed – you may be sad (experiencing an emotion) and you proceed to contemplate on relationship concerns (you go through cognition) and then you proceed to go for a run to clear your mind (you take an action). In this case, the equation would be:

EMOTION (SADNESS) + cognition (I need to go for a run) = action

CONSCIOUS + UNCONSCIOUS behavior

Consciousness is an awareness of our internal thoughts and feelings and it also has to do with proper perception for and the processing of information gathered from our surroundings. A big portion of our behaviors is through the guided unconscious processes that surround us. Like an iceberg, there is a huge amount of hidden information and only a small fraction of it is obvious to our naked eye.

Overt + Covert behavior

Overt behavior focuses on the aspects of behavior that can be observed by the naked eye. These behaviors are such as body movements, or as some would call it–interactions.

Physiological processes such as facial expressions, blushing, smiling and pupil dilation may be subtle but it all can still be seen. Covert expressions are thoughts or cognition, feelings which are emotions and responses that are not easily or visibly seen. These subtle changes in our body's responses are usually not seen by the observer's eye.

If we want to observe covert responses, then physiological or biometric sensors are usually used to help in observing them.

Rational + irrational behaviors

Any action, cognition, or emotion which is guided or influenced by reason is considered rational behavior. Irrational behavior, in contrast, is any action, emotion, or cognition that is not objectively logical. For example, people who have extreme phobias are considered as having irrational fears, which are fears that are cause them to behave a certain way.

Voluntary + involuntary behaviors

When an action is self-determined or driven by decisions and desires, this is often categorized as voluntary actions. Involuntary on the other action would be actions that are done without intent, by force, or done in an attempt to prevent it. People who are in cognitive-behavioral psychotherapy are often exposed to problematic scenarios involuntary as a form of therapy so that they can help get through this fear with the help of the therapist at hand. Now that we have a form of understanding of human behaviors, here is how we can interpret these behaviors. Keep in mind that these are just the surface or basic ways that interpretation can be done as there are more other complex and detailed ways.

#1 Establish a baseline

When you read people, you would notice that they all have unique patterns and quirks of behavior. Some people look at the floor while talking, or they have a habit of crossing their arms, some clear their throat ever so often while some pout, jiggle, or squint even. However, these actions could also mean anger, deception, or nervousness. When reading people, we first need to form a baseline by understanding context and also what normal behavior is for this person.

#2 Look for behavior deviations

When you have established baseline behaviors, your next goal is to pay close attention to the inconsistencies that show up between the baseline mannerisms and the person's words and gestures. Say for example you've noticed that your teammate usually twirls their hair when they are nervous. As your teammate starts their presentation, they start to do this. Is this common behavior in your teammate's mannerisms or is there more than meets the eye? You might want to do a little bit more digging and probe a little bit more than you normally would.

#3 Start noticing a collection of gestures

A solitary word or gesture does not necessarily mean anything but when there are a few behavioral patterns that start forming, you need to pay attention to them. It could be that your teammate starts clearing their throat in combination with twirling their hair. Or they keep shifting. This is where you need to proceed with caution.

#4 Compare and contrast

So we go back to the teammate again and you've noticed that they are acting more odd than usual. You move your observation a little closer to see when and if your teammate repeats this behavior with other people in your group. Observe how they interact with the rest of the people in the room and how their expression changes, if at all. Look at their body language and their posture.

#5 Reflect

This reflection isn't about meditation rather it is to reflect the other person's state of mind. As human beings, we have mirror neurons that act like built-in monitors wired to read another person's body language simply because we have these mannerisms as well. For example, a smile activates the smile muscles in our faces whereas a frown activates the frown muscles. When we see someone that we like, our facial muscles relax, our eyebrows arch, our blood flows to our lips making them full and our head tilts. However, if your partner does not mirror this set of behavior, then it could be that they are sending a clear message which is they are not as happy to see you.

#6 identifying the resonant voice

You might think that the most powerful person is the one that sits at the head of the table or the one that is standing in the front. That is not always the case. The most confident person always has a stronger voice and they are more likely the most powerful one. Just by looking at them, you can deduce they have an expansive posture, they have a big smile, and a strong voice. However, make no mistake that a loud voice is not a strong one. If you are presenting to an audience or pitching an idea to a group of people, you would normally focus on the leader. What happens when the leader has a weak personality? They will depend on others to make a decision and they are easily influenced by them. So when pitching or presenting to a group, identify the strong voice and you'll have a stronger chance of success.

#7 Observe how they walk

People who shuffle along or lack a flowing motion in their movements or always keep their head down while walking lack self-confidence. If you see this exhibited by a member of your team, you might be inclined to make extra effort to recognize their contribution to building this person's confidence. You might also need to ask them more direct questions at meeting so that they are inclined to offer their ideas out in the open as opposed to keeping them quiet.

#8 Using action words

Words are usually the closest way for people to understand what is going on in another person's mind. These words symbolize the thoughts that are running through their mind and in identifying these words, you also identify their meaning. Say for example if your friend says 'I decided to make this work', the action word used here is 'Decided'. This solitary word shows that your friend is 1 – not impulsive, 2 – went through a process of weighing the pros and cons, and 3 – Took time to think things through. These actions words offer insight into how a person processes a scenario and thinks.

#9 look for personality clues

Each one of us human beings has a unique personality and these rudimentary classifications can enable us to assess and relate to another person. It also helps us read someone accurately. In looking for clues, you can ask:

• Did this person exhibit more introverted or extroverted behavior?

• Do they seem driven by significance or relationships?

• How do they handle risks and uncertainty?

• What drives them or feeds their ego?

• What kinds of mannerisms does this person exhibit when they are stressed?

• What are the types of mannerisms shown when they are relaxed?

By observing a person long enough, you can pinpoint their base behaviors and mannerisms and set apart the odd one out.

CHAPTER 12
READING PEOPLE THROUGH THEIR HANDWRITING

E-very person's handwriting is known to be as unique as their personality. You can make an in-depth analysis of everything from their behavior to personality to the thought process. Graphology is the science of studying an individual's personality through how they write. Handwriting goes beyond putting a few characters on paper. It is about glimpsing into an individual's mind to decipher what they are thinking and how they are feeling based on their handwriting.

Here are some little-known secrets about speed reading a person through their handwriting.

Reading Letters of the Alphabet

How a person writes his or her letters offer a huge bank of information about their personality, subconscious thoughts, and behavioral characteristics. There are several ways of writing a single letter and every person has a distinct way of constructing it.

For example, putting a dot on the lower case "I" is an indication of an independent-spirited personality, originality, and creative thinking. These folks are organized, meticulous, and focused on details. If the dot is represented by an entire circle, there are pretty good chances of the person being more childlike and thinking outside the box. How a person constructs their upper case "I" reveals a lot about how they perceive themselves. Does their "I" feature the same size as the other letters or is it bigger/smaller compared to other letters?

A person who constructs a large "I" is often egoistic, self-centered, overconfident, and even slightly cocky. If the "I" is the size of other letters or even smaller than other letters, the person is more self-assured, positive, and happy by disposition.

Similarly, how people write their lower case "t" offers important clues into their personality. If the "t" is crossed with a long line, it can be an indication of determination, energy, passion, zest, and enthusiasm. On the other hand, a brief line across the "t" reveals a lack of empathy, low interest, and determination. The person doesn't have very strong views about anything and is generally apathetic. If a person crosses their "t" really high, they possess an increased sense of self-worth and generally have ambitious objectives.

Similarly, people who cross their "t" low may suffer from low self-esteem, low confidence, and lack of ambition. A person who narrows the loop in lower case "e" is likelier to be uncertain, suspicious, and doubtful of people. There is an amount of skepticism involved that prevents them from being trustworthy of people. These people tend to have a guarded, stoic, withdrawn, and reticent personality. A wider loop demonstrates a more inclusive and accepting personality. They are open to different experiences, ideas, and perspectives.

Next, if an individual writes their "o" to form a wide circle, they are most likely people who very articulate, expressive, and won't hesitate to share secrets with everyone. Their life is like an open book. On the contrary, a closed "o" reveals that the person has a more private personality and is reticent by nature.

Cursive Writing

Cursive writing gives us clues about people that we may otherwise miss through regular writing. It may offer us a more comprehensive and in-depth analysis of an individual's personality.

How does a person construct their lower case cursive "I?" If it has a narrow loop, the person is mostly feeling stressed, nervous, and anxious. Again, a wider loop can be a sign that the individual doesn't believe in going by the rule book. There is a tendency to rewrite the rules. They are laidback, low on ambition, and easy-going.

Again, consider the way a person writes cursive "y" to gain more information about their personality. The length and breadth of the letter "y" can be extremely telling. A thinner and slimmer "y" can be an indication of a person who is more selective about their friend circle. On the other hand, a thicker "y" reveals a tendency to get along with different kinds of people. These are social beings who like surrounding themselves with plenty of friends.

A long "y" is an indication of travel, adventure, thrills, and adventures. On the other hand, a brief cursive "y" reflects a need to seek comfort in the familiar. They are most comfortable in their homes and other known territories. A more rounded "s" is a signal of wanting to keep their near and dear ones happy. They'll always want their loved ones to be positive and cheerful.

They will seldom get into confrontations and strive to maintain a more balanced personality. A more tapering "s" indicates a curious, and hard-working personality.

They are driven by ideas and concepts. Notice how cursive "s" broadens at the lower tip. This can be a strong indication of the person being dissatisfied with their job, interpersonal relationships, and or life in general. They may not pursue their heart's true desires.

Letter Size

This is a primary observation that is used for analyzing a person through their handwriting. Big letters reveal that the person is outgoing, affable, gregarious, and extrovert. They are more social by nature and operate with a mistaken sense of pride. There is a tendency to pretend to be something they aren't. On the contrary, tiny letters can indicate a timid, reticent, introverted, and shy personality. It can indicate deep concentration and diligence. Midsized letters mean that an individual is flexible, adjusting, adaptable, and self-assured.

Gaps between Text

People who leave a little gap in between letters and words demonstrate a fear of leading a solitary life. These people always like to be surrounded by other folks and often fail to respect the privacy and personal space of other people. People who space out their words/letters are original thinkers and fiercely independent. For them, they place a high premium on freedom and independence. There is little tendency for being overwhelmed by other people's ideas, opinions, and values.

Letter Shapes

Look at the shape of an individual's letters while decoding their personality. If the writing is more rounded and in a looped manner, the person tends to be high on inventiveness and imagination! Pointed letters demonstrate that a person is more aggressive and intelligent. The person is analytical, rational, and a profound thinker. Similarly, if the letters of an alphabet are woven together, the individual is methodical, systematic, and orderly. They will rarely work or live in chaos.

Page Margin

If you thought it's only about writing, think again. Even the amount of space people leave near the edge of the margin determines their personality. Someone who leaves a big gap on the right side of the margin is known to be nervous and apprehensive about the future. People who write all over the page are known to have a mind full of ideas, concepts, and thoughts. They are itching to do several things at once and are constantly buzzing with ideas.

Slant Writing

Some people show a marked tendency for writing with a clear right or left slant while other people write impeccably straight letters. When a person's letters slant towards the right, he or she may be affable, easy-going, good-natured, and generally positive. These people are flexible, open to change, and always keen on building new social connections.

Similarly, people who write slanting letters that lean towards the left are mostly introverts who enjoy their time alone. They aren't very comfortable being in the spotlight and are happy to let others hog the limelight. Straight handwriting indicates rational, level-headed, and balanced thinking. The person is more even-tempered, grounded, and ambivalent.

There is a tiny pointer here to avoid reading people accurately. For left-handed people, the analysis is the opposite. When left-handed people have their letters slanting to the right, they are shy, introverted, and reserved. However, if their letters slant to the left, they may be outgoing, gregarious, and social extroverts.

Writing Pressure

The intensity with which an individual writes is also an indicator of their personality. If the handwriting is too intense and full of pressure (there is indentation), the individual may be fiery, aggressive, obstinate, and volatile. They aren't very open to other people's ideas, beliefs, and opinions. There is a tendency to be rigid about their views.

On the contrary, if a person writes with little pressure or intensity, they are likely to be empathetic, sensitive, and considerate towards other people's needs. These people tend to be kind, enthusiastic, passionate, lively, and intense.

Signature

A person's signature reveals plenty about an individual's personality. If it isn't comprehensible, it is a sign that he or she doesn't share too many details about themselves. They fiercely guard their private space and are reticent by nature. On the contrary, a more conspicuous and legible signature is an indication of a self-assured, flexible, transparent, assured, confident, and satisfying personality. They are generally content with what they've accomplished and displayed a more positive outlook on life.

Some people scrawl their signature quickly, which can be an indication of them being impatient, restless, perpetually in a hurry, and desiring to do multiple things at one time. A carefully written and neatly-organized signature is an indication of the person being diligent, well-organized, and precision-oriented.

Signatures that finish in an upward stroke demonstrate a more confident, fun-loving, ambitious, and goal-oriented personality. These people thrive on challenges and aren't afraid of chasing these dreams. Similarly, signatures that finish with a downward stroke are an indication of a personality that is marked by low self-esteem, lack of self-confidence, low ambition, and a more inhibited personality. These folks are likelier to be bogged down by challenges and may not be too goal-oriented.

Stand Out Writing

If a particular piece of writing stands out from the other text, look at it carefully to understand an individual's personality.

For example, if the text is generally written in a more spread out and huge writing, with only some parts of the text stuck together, the person may most likely be an uncertain, dishonest, or mistrustful individual, who is trying to conceal some important information.

Concluding

Though studying an individual's handwriting can offer you accurate insights about his or her personality, it isn't completely fool-proof. Several other factors are to be taken into consideration to analyze a person accurately. It has its shortcomings and flaws. At times, people may write in a hurried manner, which can impact their writing. Similarly, the way people construct their resume or application letter may dramatically vary from how they may write a to-do list or love letter.

If you want an accurate reading of someone's personality, consider different personality analysis methods like reading verbal and non-verbal communication techniques. Various techniques may offer you a highly in-depth, insightful, precise, and comprehensive method of understanding a person's inherent personality.

CHAPTER 13
WHAT IS BODY "MIRRORING"?

One of the critical roles of mirroring the body language of the target person is that it alerts them that you are taking a deliberate interest in the person and want to strike a rapport with the person. Mirroring helps create a connection between the participating parties in a conversation. Akin to any other aspect of communication, one needs to learn the right way of mirroring body language to realize the maximum benefits of the concept.

First, start by building your connection through fronting. In fronting, you want to lend the other person, complete attention. Go ahead and square your body so that you are directly facing the target person and try to make them the focus of your universe. Then establish eye contact, which may first appear invasive. Eye contact is critical in communicating your level of interest in the target person by communicating that you are giving undivided attention. Eye contact is also thought to elicit warm feelings that enhance a close connection. You should go ahead and initiate the triple nod, which does two functions. When one does the triple nod, then the target person is likely to speak three or four times longer, making them feel that they are being listened to or what they are communicating is important. Additionally, if one nods, then it communicates that you are in tandem with what the person is saying, and this creates a receptive environment for sustained communication. One should elicit questions that will invite nodding. For instance, start by asking if the weather is warm. Then, pretend, followed by not pretending. In this instance, you are fronting the target person and initiating the right eye contact, and applying the triple nod will help strike a rhythm with the individual. In this instance, you are likely feeling a strong connection, but to realize its full benefit try using the power of imagination by pretending the target person is the most interesting individual you have ever met. Try to imagine it and act accordingly followed by ceasing the pretense. In all this, significant levels of mirroring are likely to happen naturally on its account, but the following techniques can help enhance the mirroring of body language to attain intended goals.

Relatedly, exploit the pace and volume as many times people think of mirroring body language as mimicking the physical actions. However, mirroring body language includes all aspects of nonverbal communication, such as pace and volume. For instance, mirroring the pace and volume of the target person's speech will help initiate a connection and rhythm between the two. If the target person is, a fast talker and loud then enhance your volume and animation and if they are soft and slow, then relax and match them at their level instead. Compared to physical actions, mimicry, pace, and volume matching are easier. Recall how you felt when one of your friends adjusted their pace and volume of speaking to match yours at those instances you probably felt that they want to hold a conversation with you.

Additionally, identify the target person punctuator. Assuming that you have been carefully paying attention to the target person, you are mirroring all this time; then you will notice their favorite punctuator that he or she uses to emphasize a point. For instance, it could be an eyebrow flash such as quickly raising the eyebrows. The punctuator could also be a form of hand gesture, such as the one certain politicians use. For instance, it could be that each time the target person insists on an issue, he or she makes a certain finger gesture, then you can encourage the individual by nodding when he or she makes the particular sign. After his or her submission, you should mimic that gesture to suggest that you align with the submitted views. In all these interactions, you will not utter a single word but are connecting and communicating with the target person.

Equally important, you should test the connection with the target person in several ways. For instance, make an overt unrelated action to the conversation and observe if it is reflected. An example is where you are giving a keynote speech, and a member of the audience comes up to you, and you discuss the similarities that he and you had with your fathers that had both participated in World War II. At that instance, while talking, you get an irritating itch on your nose that you quickly scratch but then you realize that he reached up and scratched up his nose all the while continuing with his story. Even though it seemed out of place, you go ahead to evaluate if the test was a fluke and a moment later, you scratch your head, and suddenly the target person does the exact thing. It appears odd, and you almost laughed aloud. It is important to avoid repeated testing as it will break the connection and make the entire exercise appear like a prank against the best of your intention. It is also necessary to only mirror positive body language and avoid mirroring negative nonverbal communication such as turning away, closing your eyes, locking with your arms folded, or looking away. Akin to any other aspect of communication, comprehensive practice is important for one to attain efficacy levels.

As indicated, mirroring helps create a rhythm with the target individual. The main intention of mirroring the nonverbal communication of the target person is to make them notice you and fall to your pace of communication—nonverbal communication. Recall your school days when in a sporting activity or a hall with a visiting school. One of the ways that you initiated a conversation was by looking directly at the eyes of the other student that you did not know, and he or she responded. You then slowed your breathing and blinking of eyes to mimic the target student until you felt as if you are talking to each other using words. All these actions constitute mirroring to create a pattern of communication nonverbally with the target person.

For instance, if you smile at a child, it is likely to smile back at you. A common example of mirroring is when you look at your baby or any baby directly in the eyes or smile at them. In most cases, the babies will replicate the same action that you paused at them. For instance, if you clap your hands, they will also clap their hands at you. Though for the case of babies, they may lack the conscious level to perceive what they are doing, it represents the efficiency of mirroring body language. Babies with difficulties reflecting your actions can suggest that something is amiss, enabling you to investigate their welfare deeper.

Compared to men, women are more likely to mirror each other with ease. It emerges that women are likely to mirror the actions of another woman enabling two strangers, women, to connect instantly. If you are a woman or have female friends, then you must have noticed that women appear to easily connect, and it is largely due to mirroring the body language of each other. For instance, if one of the women adjusts her hair, then the other is also likely to the same, and all these increase the likelihood of striking a rapport and creating a rhythm.

It is important to take into consideration your relationship with the target person when mirroring. When mirroring the target person's actions remember that the power relationship between the two of you. For instance, mirroring your supervisor may not be a good idea. At the same time, mirroring a colleague of the opposite sex may be misinterpreted to mean that you are attempting to flirt with them even if they are responding to the mimicry. Similarly, mirroring in some contexts may appear unprofessionally and a violation of work ethics. For instance, a teacher mirroring a student or a doctor mirroring a patient may appear as a mockery even if that is not the intention. Overall, the power relationship with the target person should mediate and moderate the level of body language mirroring.

As such, mirroring body language is an efficient way of building trust and understanding fast. From all these what we learn is that mirroring body language helps initiate trust between two people, especially where the two have a passive history of interaction. As indicated earlier on, you might use mirroring body language during a random interaction such as a sporting event, a party, and any social function where you want to initiate communication and rhythm of communication to build a long-term relationship. In a way, mirroring body language acts as a technique of testing waters before one can verbalize their intentions. Chances are that if the mirroring of body language backfires then the person is likely to the walkway and make the target individual understand it was just a prank or casual moment, but if mirroring body language elicits positive responses then the two individuals are likely to go ahead and connect.

Lastly, like any other form of communication, the feelings of the target person should be taken into consideration. Even though mirroring of body language is a nonverbal and mostly passive form of nonverbal communication, a human being is an emotional creature, and it is necessary to listen and respond to the feelings of each other. For instance, if the body language of the target person indicates anger, then you should cease or adjust your actions to show consideration and care for the affected person. If the target person that you are mirroring body language is happy, then you should also exhibit positive emotions to increase the shared ground spectrum and encourage the person to exude more positive emotions.

CHAPTER 14
HOW TO USE "MIRRORING" TO IMPROVE YOUR EMPATHY

Mirroring someone else's body language is something we all do automatically, especially if we want to make a connection with them. Smile and the world smile with you are closer to the truth than you might imagine. Have you ever felt happy about something, glad to be alive, and walked through the streets with a smile on your face? Did you notice how many people smiled back at you and maybe initiated a conversation? Smiling, like yawning, is a facial expression we all seem to copy without thinking. We might even start talking like them without realizing.

Why do we do it?

Some studies have shown that we have a neuron, which controls the recognition of faces, and it is this neuron, which makes us mirror others' expressions. It is a bonding tool and by mirroring others' emotions, it makes the other person feel as if you are empathic and understand how they are feeling.

Even as early as the womb, the baby's heartbeat beats in rhythm with its mother's. As soon as we are born we begin mirroring the facial expressions and body positions we see. If our mother smiles on our faces, we are more likely to smile back. How often have you heard someone say to someone else, "You reminded me of your mother/father?" This is because the mannerisms were the same, copied from an early age. It's how we learn our native tongue and develop a local accent. We are bonded into a group identity, which can be assumed in any situation to integrate us within a new group, or even a new one-on-one relationship or conversation.

Of course, it can also work the other way. A baby or toddler feels validated when his parent mirrors his facial expression. So, the mother might say to the baby, "Are you giving me a smile?" and mirror the action. It is in this way that the child learns what the expression is. Without this skill, the child is less able to relate to others and may not develop the emotion of empathy and so is less like to form well-grounded relationships. This is because that when we form relationships we look for things we have in common with others. Similarities help us to form a bond, which is normally reflected in facial expressions and body language. If this is lacking, then it becomes more difficult to find a rapport with others.

Copycat

If a man does this with a woman, she is likely to think that he is caring and intelligent but don't try and fake it and go overboard because it could end up being farcical. Can you imagine yourself suddenly adopting an Irish accent for instance? Nevertheless, you might subconsciously notice you have a bit of a twang without even trying. However, you might more easily assume the same body position so if she leans forward on the table, you do the same. If she rests her face on her hands, you do it too.

It's also true that if you adopt a particular body position, say standing with your legs apart, you are likely to start experiencing the associated emotion, so you would begin to feel more confident. Crossing the fingers, which is putting the fingertips of each hand together, shows that the person is confident and relaxed. To effect this emotion, assume this position with your hands and the emotion will become real.

Try to become more aware not just of other people's body language and positions but your own because you can control what messages you are sending out to others. Notice if they copy you. If they do, it means that they want to get closer to you and are trying to understand what you are feeling.

Getting the Girl

Of course, this all changes if a man is in the courtship phase with a woman. If a couple is in love it is quite common for them to mirror each other's actions. They will assume the same body language and facial expressions. The closer the couple becomes, the more language is mirrored. Even when you are trying to impress someone who you would like to be closer to, this is a useful tactic to employ. Drink when they drink, smile at the same time and they will believe that you have a lot going on and that you just seem so right together and clicked. Put on some music in the background. The beat of the music should mean that you both start tapping your feet at the same time or move with the same rhythm.

The longer a couple stays together, the more likely they are to start looking like each other. Because they are using the same facial muscles to reflect the other, their muscles start developing similarly. If the mirroring declines over time and turns into a grimace the relationship is more likely to break down. And it will be the one who has more positive facial expressions who is more likely to notice the decline.

Beware of the Situation

Be aware of who you are with when your body starts mimicking theirs. If you are with your boss and your body is doing the same as theirs, they might think you are impertinent or full of yourself. On the other hand, if you are dealing with some jumped up, a pompous fool who thinks that they are better than you go ahead and copy their body language. It will throw them off but be prepared to run too!

Interviews

For instance, if you are going for an interview, quite often interviewers believe they have to adopt a closed, non-committed appearance, which does not reveal their thoughts. They do this so that the interview is not biased towards any candidate and so that everyone receives a fair chance. When you enter the room, be aware that this might be the case and try not to mimic their body language. It will send out the wrong impression. Instead, remember to display open body language. Go in there smiling and make lots of eye contact. If you are convincing, they will begin to adapt your body language and you will know that the interview is going well.

As you gain their confidence and attention, and their body language starts to relax, introduce some mirror images of their body language. If you get them onside you will be able to recognize this, and they will be more likely to help you get what you want: the job, the promotion, the raise.

Crowd Pleasers

It is not unusual for a whole crowd to copy one person's actions. Fans at a concert may leave their seats to stand at the front rather than be the only person sitting. Stadium spectators will start a wave reaction. Studies have been done to show that people will copy others so that they do not stand out in a crowd. For instance, in a waiting room, if one person took a ticket and then threw it away someone watching might assume that they had to do it too. There might be no obvious reason why, but they may sit there and suppose it triggered some mechanism for instance to place them in a queue. When others witnessed this, they followed suit until everyone who entered was taking a ticket from a machine and throwing it away. All for no reason.

If you want to build a strong report, mirroring is a super powerful way to do it and can improve your relationships across the board. Do it to someone you already know well and see what a difference it can make. It is such a strong tool that it might be best to practice before you try for that promotion using it

CHAPTER 15
HOW TO SPOT INSECURITY

When Someone behaves Irrationally, you have to remind yourself that this could be because they are acting out of a certain emotion, or it also could be that their insecurity is behind this false sense of bravado. When you notice this, you will more likely procure a sense of empathy for these people who act arrogantly or rudely since what they are trying to do is cover their insecurity.

Your ability to spot insecurity can be advantageous to you in several situations. Negotiation, conflict resolution, and even within a problem-solving dynamic. Insecurity can be about anything—looks, power, money, smartness, getting better grades, and so on—and most of these insecurities creep out from a sense of material value Once you do though, it gives you leverage that you can use to connect with the person on a level which they can relate to. In a negotiation situation, this can be extremely useful in swinging the odds into your favor.

Being able to spot insecurity is also going to serve you well in terms of protecting yourself. Sometimes, these insecure individuals have strong, negative energy about them, and it is easy to get swept up in their emotional turmoil and become insecure yourself if you spend enough time around them. A lack of eye contact, nervous pacing, hunched posture, biting of the fingernails in some cases, repeatedly touching certain parts of the body like the neck, and fidgeting are obvious signs of insecurity and discomfort. Aside from the obvious body language that they display, keep your eyes peeled for the following signs that signal you're dealing with an insecure individual:

- **They Make You Feel Insecure Too** - Their insecurity will be so strong it starts to rub off on you. You'll want to exercise caution here, since beginning to doubt yourself is going to make you easy prey to manipulators.

- **Constant Worry** - They're constantly worried that every decision they make is going to reflect badly on them. They express concern about not knowing what the right thing to do is. They ask you what you think several times, or even what you think they should do. They might apologize for being indecisive and unable to decide just yet.

- **Showing Off** - Insecurity could also manifest itself in a different manner, where the insecure individual feels a constant need to show off their accomplishments just to make themselves feel better. Constantly brag about their amazing lifestyle, their wonderful shoes, their huge cars, and their elite education. All of this is done to convince themselves that they have it all in a poor attempt to feel better about themselves.

- **Becoming Defensive** - Insecure people become even more nervous, jittery, and on edge when they feel like they are being ganged up on or pressured into deciding. They'll be worried about offending you or making you angry with some of the choices they make, but they may become defensive if they feel like they're being attacked.

- **Frequent Complaints** - There's always something to complain about when the whole world doesn't seem right to the insecure individual. They'll spend hours, days, weeks, or even months mulling over the concerns and worries, and find it hard to escape that "negative funk" they're in, no matter how much you try to coax them out of it. Even when there's nothing to complain about, they'll be the ones to find something wrong.

- **Indecisive Nature** - They find it nearly impossible to make a decision and stick to it. They'll second guess, question, bounce from one choice to the next, and keep asking the same question repeatedly, almost as if they're having a hard time accepting the answers they're being given. Even if you gave them a possible solution, they'll reject your initial suggestion, but then come back and circle it again.

Mastering your emotions is essential to dealing with an insecure individual to avoid being easily influenced by their volatile, unpredictable emotional state. Compassion and empathy are especially important, what the insecure person needs are someone who can understand what they're going through. Not someone who is there to judge, criticize, or ridicule. Compassion requires a balanced approach so that our negative emotions are either exaggerated or suppressed when dealing with an insecure individual. This balancing act comes out from the process of relating our personal experiences with that of the suffering of others. Your ability to analyze their body language and read the unspoken communication that goes on is going to be your best asset in a time like this.

Insecurity is an emotional state that arises following a situation that is perceived as alarming or threatening. If the person confronted with this stimulus feels that their resources or skills are insufficient to manage and/or overcome the situation, they are likely to feel insecure. This emotion may manifest itself in the form of higher levels of anxiety, psychomotor agitation, allowing the person to feel unnerved but still able to mobilize extra resources to enable him to succeed. In these cases, insecurity has a protective effect in that it prevents us from making mistakes or taking unnecessary risks. For example, when one of the couples feels that their relationship is not safe, they can implement some strategies that, in their eyes, imply the solidification of the relationship, such as the promotion of dialogue, romantic outings, or even psychotherapeutic follow-up. Similarly, when a worker perceives his or her place as being at risk of being laid off, he or she will seek alternatives to avoid unemployment. But both in one context and the other insecurity can assume a higher level of intensity, no longer having such a protective effect.

These cases, though are likely to be dominated by irrational beliefs, which grow spirally and produce a blocking effect. The person starts to live by what makes him insecure without, however, being able to find adjusted solutions. In the first example, this state of anxiety could translate into a set of behaviors that have both despair and nonsense, such as starting to search the partner's cell for signs of a potential extramarital relationship, aggressive and/or controlling comments, etc. In the following example, it could happen that the person would be so depressed that he would not invest either in the current job or in the search for the new placement, allowing insecurity to have the blocking effect.

What clues or signs are evidenced by someone insecure? How can we identify him?

The most insecure people are overwhelmed by fear, and as a result, it is usually more difficult for them to take an assertive stance, that is, they have very serious difficulties in expressing clearly and honestly what they think and what they feel. Within a group, both can strive to go unnoticed as they can make efforts to please everyone. In practice, they feel an intense fear of failing, of not meeting expectations, of not being up to it. Some people are very confident in professional terms and are more insecure in relational/affective terms. In the same way, some people feel safe and comfortable in the performance of roles related to effective relationships but which reveal serious insecurities in other areas of life. It may not be easy to recognize the most insecure people, especially if the analysis is superficial.

Sometimes it is easier for an insecure individual to recognize another who shares the same insecurities, as he is more aware and more attentive to certain details that will go along with the majority.

Factors Determining Good and Bad

None of these traits helps us to behave virtuously. There is a thin line between being insecure and being a brat. Here are some identifying factors that can help you separate the good and the bad:

1. Self-kindness is not self-judgment.

Compassion towards someone insecure is being understanding and warm to them when they fail, or when we suffer, or at moments when we feel inadequate. We should not be ignoring these emotions or criticizing. People who have compassion understand that being human comes with its imperfections and failing is part of the human experience. There will inevitably be no failure when we attempt something because failure is part of learning and progress.

Things cannot be exactly the way it should be or supposed to be or how we dream it to be. There will be changes and when we accept this with kindness and sympathy and understanding, we experience greater emotional equanimity.

2. Common humanity and not isolation

It is a common human emotion to feel frustrated especially when things do not go the way we envision them to. When this happens, frustration is usually accompanied by irrational isolation, making us feel and think that we are the only person on earth going through this or making dumb mistakes like this. News flash—all humans suffer, all of us go through different kinds of suffering at varying degrees. Compassion involves recognizing that we all suffer and all of us have personal inadequacies. It does not happen to 'Me' or 'I' alone.

3. Mindfulness is not over-identification.

Compassion needs us to be balanced with our approach so that our negative emotions are neither exaggerated nor suppressed. This balancing act comes out from the process of relating our personal experiences with that of the suffering of others. This puts the situation we are going through into a larger perspective.

We need to keep mindful awareness so that we can observe our negative thoughts and emotions with clarity and openness. Having a mindful approach is non-judgmental and it is a state of mindful reception that enables us to observe our feelings and thoughts without denying them or suppressing them. There is no way that we can ignore our pain and feel compassion at the same time. By having mindfulness, we also prevent the over-identification of our thoughts and feelings.

Discovering Compassion

You're so dumb! You don't belong here, loser! Those jeans make you look like a fat cow! You can't sit with us! It's safe to say we've all heard some kind of rude, unwanted comments either directly or indirectly aimed at us. Would you talk like this to a friend? Again, the answer is a big NO.

Believe it or not, it is a lot easier and natural for us to be kind and nice to people than to be mean and rude to them whether it is a stranger or someone we care about in our lives. When someone we care about is hurt or is going through a rough time, we console them and say it is ok to fail. We support them when they feel bad about themselves and we comfort them to make them feel better or just to offer a shoulder to cry on.

We are all good at being understanding and compassionate and kind to others. How often do we offer this same kindness and compassion to ourselves? Research on self-compassion shows that those who are compassionate are less likely to be anxious, depressed, or stressed, and more resilient, happy, and optimistic. In other words, they have better mental health.

Identifying Someone with Insecurity

Insecure people tend to spread their negativity and self-doubt to others as well and here is how you can identify them and decide whether to show compassion or to show them the exit:

Insecure people try to make you feel insecure yourself.

You start questioning your ability and self-worth and this happens when you are around a specific person. This individual can manipulate you and talk about their strengths and how they are good in this and that and in a way try to put you down. They project their insecurities on you.

Insecure people need to showcase his or her accomplishments.

Inferiority is at the very core of their behavior and for people like this, compassion to tell them that they are not what they think in their heads is just a waste of your time. They feel insecure and to hide it, talk about their accomplishments, not in a good way but constantly brag about their amazing lifestyle, their wonderful shoes, their huge cars, and their elite education. All this is done to convince themselves that they do have it all and you have none.

People who are insecure drops the "humblebrag" far too much.

The humblebrag is essentially a brag that is disguised as a self-derogatory statement. In this social media age, you can see plenty of humblebrags who complain about their first-world problems such as all the travel they need to do or the amount of time they spend watching their kids play and win games or even the person who complains about having a tiny pimple when the rest of their face looks flawless. Social media is ripe with narcissistic people, and this is not worth your time. Do not feel any less just because someone shows off how much traveling they need to do.

Insecure people frequently complain that things aren't good enough.

They like showing off the high standards that they have, and while you may label them as snobs, it might be a harder feeling to shake off because you might be thinking that they are better than you although you know that it is all an act. They proclaim their high standards to assert that they are doing better than everyone else and make you feel less of yourself and more miserable. Pay no attention to people like this.

How to Spot a Dangerous Person

There are always people at the extremes of each trait and, sometimes, these people can be dangerous. While most people exhibit a fair few 'good' personality traits, and perhaps a couple of 'bad' ones, some people exhibit a singular bad trait so strongly or even several bad traits at a low level. Such people can be anything from mildly annoying, lacking in social skills, to downright manipulative or abusive. Most concerning is the fact that some people can mask these negative traits quite well. How many times have you met someone you thought was friendly enough, only to realize later that they are not someone you want to know at all? What about friends you have who act one way in one situation but can be completely different at other times? Everyone would do well to remember that no matter how good we get at analyzing and speed-reading others, there is always a chance that something important will escape our notice, or that the other person will be able to mask their intentions too well.

Despite this, there are some red flags for which we can learn to watch out. These apply to all of our relationships – not just romantic ones. Identifying personality types that may do us harm involves understanding what healthy relationships look like, whether they are with family members, friends, colleagues, superiors, and yes, romantic or sexual partners. Here is a list of some telltale signs that something's wrong in your interaction with another person. Their behavior points to their personality – and if their personality is harming you, then you are always within your rights to step back, get out, and look for support to ensure your safety, physically, emotionally, and mentally. Identifying one of these red flags in your relationship with someone doesn't mean you have to cut ties with them immediately, but it should give you pause about how you'd like things to change in the future.

CHAPTER 16
HOW TO SHOW DOMINANCE THROUGH BODY LANGUAGE

People who want to imply being in charge usually use dominant nonverbal cues. These people may not be aware of these body language signals may not even be aware that they are doing so and may just be a factor in their dominant personality.

Used properly, showing dominance through body language can help you gain respect and popularity, a method usually employed by politicians during the campaign period. Here are some actions that express dominance.

Appearing Larger

Appearing larger and more powerful is an important factor in showing dominance, and this can be traced back to man's prehistoric roots. This action is also very evident in animals, where fights for dominance are often settled by size comparison, saving the parties involved from altercations.

This behavioral bias was inherited by modern humans and can be seen practiced when competing with others. Using the same size and body language signal, they try to show their superiority by appearing to be threatening and should be avoided. Here are examples of these size signals:

Make Your Body Appear Bigger

A bigger person is often seen as more dominant and more threatening. If you have the height advantage, then good for you because you are already large, and this effect comes naturally to you. It's one of the main reasons why taller people tend to be more successful than others, not only in sports but also in the corporate world. For the smaller ones, here are some gestures, postures, and body language tricks to appear bigger.

Place your hand on your hips. This will make you appear wider than you usually are, thus adding to your size.

Stand upright. Straightening your back can add inches to your height.

Sit or stand with your legs apart. This applies to men, and like placing your hands on your hips, it also adds to your 'width.'

Hold your head and chin up. Another technique you can use to add to your height.

Stand Higher

When you are standing higher than the other person, you are in a more dominant position giving you a natural advantage. You can do this by:

Stand while the other party sits. This instantly gives you the height advantage.

Stand on a platform or step to give you extra height when compared with the other party

Stand tall and straight. Tiptoe if you must.

Wear a large hat or wear high heel shoes.

Style your hair to make you look taller. This is common practice with women.

Remember, people who make themselves appear larger or bigger aim to be more dominant, threatening, or powerful.

Claiming Territory

Humans are quite territorial, thanks to our ancestral origins and heritage. People shot a lot of territorial signals, and you can use these to predict behavior. When trying to be more dominant, you can do the following nonverbal signals to claim territory:

Claim a particular area in a conference room, exhibition center, meeting room, or office room and expect other people to comply with the rules you set for that area.

Invade the personal space of the other person to imply dominance. You can even emphasize the act with a touch like lightly holding the arm or patting the person's back, which indicates ownership. A study showed that a show of affection may not always be the reason when a man touches a woman. Instead, it can be a show of dominance or ownership.

Invade an area currently owned by the other person. You can sit at the edge of that person's table or on their chair, which is a common gesture of dominance. This move is often used by power-tripping managers or bosses who invade other people's territory to show them who is in charge.

Touch or hold the other person's possessions. When this gesture is made with a relaxed composure, this implies that you own what they own, which is another indication of domination. You may pick the other person's favorite pen or phone or rearrange their desk. It's like saying, 'what's yours is also mine, and you can't do anything to stop me.'

Walk in the center of the corridor so that other people stay out of your way. This is a claim to a common territory, which implies authority and dominance over others. The same can be observed from some drivers during heavy traffic wherein they don't let other drivers merge into their lane.

When the meeting room has a long table, sit at one end. This position is usually reserved for someone with a superior role or power. Sitting here emphasizes your dominance over others.

When talking with a group, position yourself at the center, which forces others to pay attention to what you're discussing. Since your back will be vulnerable, ensure that the persons you trust are behind you.

Signaling Superiority

There are various direct or indirect power cues that you can show if you want to appear dominant, particularly in social contexts. You can either plan these signals or improvise when the need arises. These power signals can be a combination of verbal and nonverbal languages. Here are some of the techniques that you can use:

Show of Dominance through Wealth

Wear expensive clothes, watch, jewelry, accessories, and makeup. Doing so makes you appear rich, powerful, and well-connected.

Show off your possessions indirectly. This can be done by paying hefty bills in a relaxed manner, flashing the latest flagship mobile phone, or driving an expensive car.

Show of Dominance through Control

Order a staff or team member to bring you something in front of another person. This implies that you are in charge of the area. For example, you can tell someone to bring you a cup of coffee, print a certain report immediately, or have them call another person and bring that person into the meeting room.

Controlling and giving orders can also be combined with a display of wealth to emphasize its importance. For example, call your secretary while in the presence of others and have her book you a business class flight, a five-star hotel with all the bells and whistles, and a chauffeured luxury car. Showing that you can get whatever you want indicates power and dominance, and this is a move usually exhibited by top corporate executives to impress their customers.

Controlling Time

No, you don't need a time machine for this technique. Similar to dominating other people's space, you can control their time as well by setting a pace for them to follow. You can use nonverbal cues to exert time pressure on other people. Here are some verbal and nonverbal techniques you can use:

Interrupt

Interrupt a discussion by leaving early or arriving late

Hurry Other People

Set a fast pace for other people to follow

Walk using wide strides. This implies you're determined a certain goal quickly and that you are confident with your actions. When you're walking with another person, walk a bit faster to set your own pace. This shows who's in charge, and the slower person will be forced to also walk fast to keep up.

Talk faster than usual. This forces others to also talk fast and give you control of their time.

Slow Down Other People

When talking with another person, interrupt him by asking for a concise and brief talk. This implies you value your time more than his. You can also use this technique when breaking a pace set by another person so you can change the discussion's focus. This may also be effective in counteracting the hurried pace of a dominant person.

Facial Expressions

To show dominance, it's important to extensively use facial expressions to show power and control. Here are some examples.

Avoid Eye Contact

To suggest that someone is not important to you, you can simply avoid looking at them.

Make Prolonged Eye Contact

When you gaze at the other person intensely while proving a point, it implies that you stand by your word, and you're not budging an inch. It also shows dominance, being uncooperative and unwilling, and being strong-minded.

Make a Neutral Face

This can be very useful during negotiations because making this facial expression can be interpreted by the other person that you are unimpressed. When you hold this facial expression while another person is pitching his product or case enthusiastically, it can cause him to buckle or be unnerved. This is often exhibited during academic debates when a domain or subject expert, such as a professor, wants to show dominance by showing that he's not interested in the other person's ideas.

Smile Sparingly

People who want to show dominance smile less often than the submissive ones. Although there's a chance that some people might dislike you, smiling less often shows you mean business and you are in control.

Display Your Crotch (Applies Only to Men)

Of course, you need to have your pants on when you do this move or risk spending the night inside the jail. Stand with your feet shoulder-width apart with both feet firmly planted on the ground. This is called standing crotch display and is a very masculine way of highlighting your genitals to show dominance or superiority. You can emphasize this move by 'adjusting' or lightly 'touching' the crotch area. You can also do this technique by sitting down by opening your legs and knees.

It's very uncommon for women to show this gesture because it can be interpreted as an invitation to sexual intimacy, although some may do so as a show of strength and equality with men.

Counteract Dominance

But what if another person in the room is showing dominance using the techniques mentioned above? You can derail their actions by utilizing these nonverbal strategies:

Return the Gaze

If the other person looks you in the eye longer than what you consider normal, look back, and return the gaze. Doing so might get you distracted by their piercing eyes, but there's a way around that. Instead of looking directly into their eyes, imagine a triangle formed by the eyes and forehead and then look at the center of that triangle.

Initiate the First Touch

Just before that person is about to touch you, touch him first. Or retaliate with your touch when he touched you. This shows that you're not one to mess with or dominate.

Take it Slow

When the dominant person is trying to rush you, breathe slowly, remain calm, and slow down the pace. This can imply that there's no need to hurry. Show that the slower pace you're trying to set is more ideal and be persistent about it. This applies to both walking and talking

Use Humor

A dominant person always aims to take over conversations. Break that dominance by telling a joke and take back control of the conversation. You can get a laugh by telling a joke or using nonverbal actions. You can use this break to shift the discussion back to your preferred topic.

Body language can be used to show dominance and influence the action of others. You can also use it to counteract imposed dominance by others.

CONCLUSION

Everything that a person does or says reveals something about their personality. Actions, beliefs, and thoughts of people are aligned perfectly with each other in a way that they all reveal the same things concerning an individual. Just as it is said that all methods can lead to Rome, everything a person thinks or does can reveal a lot about their personality makeup and personality. Words that are spoken by a person, even if they carry less weight, tell a great deal about a person's insecurities and desires.

No one doubts that the words we speak or write are a full expression of our inner personalities and thoughts. However, beyond the real content of a language, exclusive insights into the minds of the author are usually hidden in the text's style.

From our acts of dominance to truthfulness, we are revealing to others too much about us. You can quickly know the most important of all the people in the room by listening to the words that they use. Confident and high-status people use very few "I" words. The higher a person's status is in a given situation, the less the "I" words they will use in their conversations.

Each time people feel confident, they tend to focus on the task that they have at hand, and not necessarily on them. "I" is also used less in the weeks that follow a given cultural upheaval. As age kicks on, we tend to use more positive emotional words and even make very fewer references to ourselves.

It is important to be true to yourself. The tips and techniques discussed in this book are not to help you become someone else. Quite the contrary. I have intended to help you let your true self shine. Regardless of what your personality is like, these tips and strategies will help you let your personality shine. People will seek you for who you are. In a dating context, anyone interested in you will do so because they can see that you are authentic and relatable. As I stated earlier, if you pretend to be someone you are not, this will eventually backfire on you.

Good luck.

BOOK 3

GASLIGHTING

How to Spot and Survive the Hidden Manipulation Others Use to Control Your Life ,recover from a toxic relationship, avoid narcissistic people.

JASON ART

INTRODUCTION

Gaslighting is a form of manipulation that involves a person deliberately creating a false environment. The primary goal of gaslighting is to create a situation that makes the victim question their own memory and perception of reality.

Gaslighting creates a feeling of anxiety or discomfort in the victim that they do not understand. They may feel like they are losing their mind, or like they are going crazy. They could even accuse the abuser of trying to make them kill themselves; however, this is not always true. Gaslighting can be used as a form of abuse in many ways.

People who have been gaslighted can relate to this kind of feeling when they are around someone who seems to be picking at their brain or appearance. This kind of behavior could be considered a form of "mind games". The person experiencing this will agree that they felt "different" or "off" around this person and sometimes feel like they are crazy for feeling the way that they do.

Gaslighting is a form of emotional abuse. It's used by narcissists in their efforts to secure power and control over others. It's a technique that allows them to wear you down and erode your confidence.

People who find themselves being gaslighted might know about gaslighting but they might not realize what it is or why it happens. The goal of this article is to provide insight into the concept of gaslighting along with facts that will help you determine whether or not you're being gaslighted and how you can protect yourself from it.

Gaslighting is a form of psychological abuse that manipulates the environment to convince people that they are not experiencing reality. It is an act designed to sow doubt, confusion, and suspicion.

Gaslighting can happen in a variety of forms:

Passive-aggressive behavior that makes a victim feel as though their actions are being questioned or criticized.

Making someone feel as though they are going crazy, making them question their own sanity.

Using a combination of tricks and manipulation to create internal conflict within people.

Here's how it starts:

At Gaslighting, we understand that our customers rely on us for their satisfaction. That's why we use only the highest quality parts and take great pride in ensuring that our customers get the best tool for their money. We understand that you want a tool that will last for years and years without failure. However, there are certain components that can fail at any time. For instance, if you were to lose your wrench or screwdriver while out on the job site, you would want to be able to use it immediately without having to wait for another one to be shipped to you. This is where the Gaslighting GASLIGHT comes in handy! The GASLIGHT allows you to use your tools immediately with no wait time! It allows you to control the rate at which your tools wear down as well as the rate at which you replace them. The GASLIGHT keeps your tools perfectly balanced so you'll never have to worry about using it again! It eliminates the need for regular adjustments and lets your tools perform at maximum capacity even when they're incredibly worn down! Be sure you keep yours on hand because it's never a good idea to leave home wiring out in the open! You never know when a storm could hit and damage one of the many electrical wires that run throughout your property! The Gaslighting GASLIGHT has 120V power which can run up to four different tools simultaneously!

What Is Gaslighting?

There is a violence that is not made of anger expressed, on the contrary, it is insidious, made up of hostile silences alternating with pungent words. It is an ancient form of abuse, perpetrated in a particular way among the "safe" domestic walls, which leaves deep psychological wounds.

The term derives from a theatrical work of 1938 Gas light (Gas lights, initially known as Angel Street in the United States), and from the film adaptations of Alfred Hitchcock "Rebecca - the first wife" of 1940 and "Angoscia" Italian film of 1944. The plot is about a husband who tries to drive his wife mad by manipulating small elements of the environment, and insisting that his wife is mistaken or badly remembers when he notices these changes. The title originates from the subtle weakening of the gas lights by the husband, something that the wife carefully notes but that the husband insists is only the fruit of her imagination.

From here, the term gaslighting is used to define a cruel manipulative behavior put in place by a person to make the other doubt about herself and her judgments of reality to the point of feeling confused, wrong.

Gaslighter is defined as the one who puts this mental manipulation into action, undermining every certainty and safety of the partner, acting like real brainwashing, which puts the victim in a position to think he deserves that punishment and to have guilt for to have been wrong.

This type of psychological violence is insidious, subtle, sometimes justified by the victim herself. It is gratuitous and persistent violence, administered in daily doses, and has the ability to "cancel" the ability to judge and evaluate the person who is the target of evaluation.

Research shows that in the vast majority of cases the victim and the gaslighter are almost always close partners or relatives.

In many cases the gaslighting behavior is adopted by the abusive spouse to punish or remove the other when there are conflicting marital relationships, personal dissatisfaction and extramarital affairs.

Gaslighting is a form of violence that also arises within relationships previously built on love. Then, it happens that frustration to which one does not know how to adequately react, undermines the security and trust that the manipulator puts in itself and everything collapses: love is replaced by gratuitous malice and harassment.

Examples of bad phrases that can come out in a conversation with these types of people:

"You're fat! (Lean, ugly, etc.) "

"Excuse me, my wife is a moron!"

"You always miss everything! You don't make a right one! "

"But how can you not remember! You told me so! "

"You never told me! You will have imagined it! "

"Your friends are insignificant, just like you!"

"If I leave you will be alone for life!"

"You are nobody!"

Messages therefore of devaluation, injunctions that hurt emotionally and the soul, even more if pronounced in the presence of other people as if it were a public humiliation. The gaslighter knows how to hurt, and feels enjoyment from the effects of its behavior.

We can identify three categories of manipulators:

a) **The fascinating.** It is probably the most insidious, subjecting its victim to a continuous Scottish shower. He alternates hostile silences and tremendous prodding with moments of flood of love and flattery. One can only imagine the atmosphere of disorientation that pervades the victim.

b) **The good boy.** Which seems to have at heart only the good of the victim but in reality it is an egoist disguised as a selfless person. He is always careful to put his own needs, his personal advantage before that of the victim, even if he manages to give an opposite impression.

c) The intimidator. It is the opposite of the previous manipulators and, certainly, the most direct. He doesn't bother hiding behind false facades. He openly blames the victim, makes sarcastic jokes about her, and explicitly attacks her.

The purpose of the gaslighting behavior, common to the three categories of manipulators, is to reduce the victim to a total level of physical and psychological dependence, annulling his capacity for autonomy and responsibility. The victim will feel as imprisoned by this behavior and, slowly, his resistances will fade to the point of disappearing completely, becoming the unconscious accomplice of his tormentor.

Then the victim will go through three successive phases:

a)   The 1st phase will be characterized by a distortion of communication. The persecuted person will no longer be able to understand the persecutor. The "dialogues" will be characterized by hostile silences, alternated by destabilizing spikes. The victim will be so disoriented, confused in the fog.

b)   The second phase will be characterized by a defense attempt. The victim will try to convince his abuser that what he says does not correspond to the truth; will try to establish a dialogue, obstinate, with the hope that this will serve to change the behavior of the gaslighter. The victim will feel as if invested in a basic task: his listening and dialogue skills will succeed in changing the abuser.

c)   The third phase is the descent into depression. The victim will be convinced that what the abuser says against him is true, resigns himself, and becomes insecure and extremely vulnerable and dependent. In this phase the relational perversion reaches its peak: violence becomes chronic and the victim is convinced of the reason and also of the goodness of the manipulator who, often, is also idealized.

And don't think that these are just inventions because this phenomenon is much more common than you might think and I want to give you some examples. Psychologist Martha Stout (2005) argues that sociopaths frequently use gaslighting tactics. Sociopaths consistently transgress social laws and conventions, and exploit others, but they are also typically credible liars who consistently deny any wrongdoing. Thus, some victims of sociopaths can doubt their perception.

Jacobson and Gottman (1998) report that some violent husbands could use gaslighting on their wives, even firmly denying that they ever committed any act of violence.

The psychologists Gass and Nichols (1988) use the term gaslighting to describe the dynamics observed between spouses in some cases of adultery. Male therapists can contribute to the discomfort of female patients by misinterpreting their behaviors. Her husband's gaslighting behaviors provide a recipe for the so-called psychological breakdown for some women and suicide in some of the worst situations.

Members of the Manson Family in the crimes committed during the late sixties entered homes without stealing anything, but moved the furniture to upset the residents.

The Effect Of Gaslighting

1.   Gaslighting can have catastrophic effects on a person's psychological health; the procedure is gradual, chipping away the person's certainty and self-esteem. They may come to accept they merit the abuse.

2.   Gaslighting can also influence a person's social life. The abuser may manipulate them into cutting ties with friends and relatives. The individual might also isolate themselves, believing they are unstable or unlovable.

3.   Especially when the person escapes the abusive relationship, the effects of gaslighting can persevere. The person may even now question their discernments and have difficulty making decisions. They are also more reluctant to voice their emotions and feelings, knowing that they are probably going to be invalidated.

4.   Gaslighting may lead a person to create mental health concerns. The constant self-uncertainty and disarray can contribute to anxiety. A person's sadness and low self-esteem may lead to despondency. Post-traumatic stress and codependency are common developments.

5.   Some survivors may battle to confide in others; they may be on constant guard for additional manipulation. The individual may criticize themselves for not catching the gaslighting earlier. Their refusal to show vulnerability might prompt strain in future relationships.

CHAPTER 1
RECOVERING FROM GASLIGHTING

Gaslighting is a secret form of abuse that blossoms with uncertainty. A person can grow to distrust everything they feel, hear, and recollect. One of the most significant things a survivor can get is validation.

The individuals who have encountered gaslighting may also wish to look for therapy. A therapist is a natural party who can aid in reinforcing one's sense of reality. In therapy, an individual can modify their self-esteem and recover command of their lives. A therapist might also treat any mental health concerns caused by the abuse, for example, PTSD. With time and backing, a person can recoup from gaslighting.

Are You Being Gaslighted?

Gaslighting may not include these experiences or feelings, but if you recognize yourself in any of them, give it additional attention.

1.   You are constantly re-thinking yourself.

2.   You ask yourself, "Am I excessively sensitive?" twelve times each day.

3.   You regularly feel confounded and even insane at work.

4.   You're continually saying 'sorry' to your mom, father, and sweetheart, boss.

5.   You wonder now and again if you are a "sufficient" sweetheart/wife/representative/companion/little girl.

6.   You can't get why, with so many beneficial things in your life, you aren't more joyful.

7.   You purchase garments for yourself, goods for your apartment, or other personal buys in light of your partner, considering what he might want rather than what might cause you to feel incredible.

8.   You often rationalize your partner's conduct to loved ones.

9.   You end up denying data of loved ones, so you don't need to clarify or rationalize.

10.   You realize something is off-base, but you can never fully communicate what it is, even to yourself.

11.   You begin lying to maintain a strategic distance from the put-downs and reality turns.

12.   You experience difficulty settling on basic decisions.

13.   You reconsider before raising blameless subjects of discussion.

14.   Before your partner gets back home, you go through a list in your mind to foresee anything you may have fouled up that day.

15.   There is a sense that you used to be a different person — increasingly sure, progressively carefree, and progressively relaxed.

16.   You begin addressing your better half through his secretary so you don't need to reveal to him things you're apprehensive about may agitate him.

17.   You feel as if you can't do anything right.

18.   Your children start attempting to shield you from your partner.

19.   You get yourself angry with people you've generally coexisted with previously.

20.   You feel sad and dreary.

Gaslighting Tends To Work In Stages

From the start, it might be generally minor—in reality, you may not see it. At the point when your partner blames you for intentionally attempting to undermine you by appearing late to his office party, you attribute it to his nerves or expect you didn't generally mean it or maybe even start to ponder whether you were attempting to undermine him—but then you let it go. Inevitably, however, gaslighting turns into a greater piece of your life, distracting your musings and overpowering your feelings.

Eventually, you're buried in full-scale sorrow, miserable and dismal, unfit even to recollect the person you used to be, with your perspective and your sense of self. You may not continue through every one of the three phases. But for many women, gaslighting goes from terrible to more awful.

Stage 1: Disbelief Stage 1 is portrayed by disbelief; your deceiver says something over the top—"That person who approached us for bearings was extremely simply attempting to get you into bed!"— And you can't exactly accept your ears. You think you've misjudged, or perhaps he has, or possibly he was simply kidding. The comment appears to be so unusual; you may ignore it. Or on the other hand, maybe you attempt to address the blunder but without a ton of energy. Possibly you even get into it a long time ago, included arguments, but you're still quite sure of your perspective. Although you'd like your deceiver's endorsement, you don't yet feel frantic for it.

Stage 2: Defense Stage 2 is set apart by the need to safeguard yourself. You scan for proof to refute your deceiver and contend with him fanatically, frequently in your mind, frantically attempting to win his endorsement.

Stage 3: Depression gaslighting is the most challenging of all: downturn. Now, you are effectively attempting to demonstrate that your deceiver is correct, because then perhaps you could do things his way and at long last win his endorsement.

How It Works

Remember that you can get away from the abuse, but there are things that can happen if you're not careful, if you continue to stay in the presence of someone who gaslights you, and who abuses you.

What can happen though/ let's talk about what can happen if you continue to suffer at the hands of a gaslighter?

Memory Loss

This is what's so scary about gaslighting. When you experience gaslighting after a while, sometimes you'll start to feel so guilty and have a lot of self-doubts that you'll tend to forget things that happened. You may not know why it happened, and not remember things that happened between those time periods. Some people will even experience the abuser accusing them of something that happened, but they're unable to actually remember what happened.

Sometimes, what's scary about gaslighting is when you experience that, over a long period of time, you'll begin to realize that you can't remember the exact situations, because your mind and reality are completely skewered. You'll start to realize that you can't remember things that the abuser would accuse you of.

Sometimes, the abuser would accuse you of things that you're doing, but you don't remember doing them, and this, in turn, will lead you to wonder whether or not you did something. You'll definitely start to realize this as well when you get away.

Sometimes, they'll claim you're abusive, and how you hurt them, but you literally can't remember why. You oftentimes will try very hard to remember the abuse and trauma, but you can't.

Another type of way you can lose your memory with this is blanking on various things. When you're gaslit, you start to feel your reality starts to change, and you start to become an effect of the abuser that's there. However, sometimes after gaslighting happens, you can't remember all of the trauma you went through.

Perhaps it's a defensive mechanism, or maybe it's just your brain trying to blackout everything terrible that happened to you. But you won't remember things. Your memory starts to become less and less, to the point where it becomes a struggle to remember it all.

You may walk around with really bad brain fog too. Abusers love to skewer your sense of reality, so when they do this, you can't remember things and your brain becomes a foggy mess as a result of this.

You Feel Constantly Guilty

One-way narcissistic abusers take you down is by making you feel guilty constantly. It isn't a pity party "oh woe is me" concept; it's more of they will make you feel bad for even existing. That's the problem with narcissistic abusers. They will make sure that you feel guilty, constantly terrible, and you're the one at fault.

Narcissistic abusers will throw jabs at you, telling you how you're nothing. They will also say that you're just worthless, a piece of trash, and you're constantly not allowed to be anything more. That's the problem with many abusers. They will oftentimes make you feel guilty, to the point where depression, even suicidal tendencies start to come up.

You wonder if you're the one to blame for everything. You start to feel like you're the one at fault, when you may not be. Even when you're out of the situation and away from it, even years down the road, it can haunt you, like a ghost that hasn't been exorcised yet.

You feel bad for even being alive and that's because your narcissistic abuser has taken you to such a lower level that you don't know what to do with yourself other than to think that hey, you are the one to blame, and you are worthless.

But of course, that isn't the case.

Isolation From Help

This is what's scary about narcissistic abusers. Remember, they will claim that you're the one who is crazy, that others are lying, that you're not the one who is right here. They will tell you that you should only believe them, and never anyone else.

Over time, when you're with an abuser like this, you can develop a Stockholm syndrome, where you know that you need to get away, but you can't isolate yourself from help, and oftentimes, even after you get it, you can't really get the help that you need.

That's because you don't trust other people. They are all liars, remember? Your abuser would tell you that, and even if you've managed to leave, that can hang around in your head.

That's why, when people who have been gaslighted leave their abusers, they sometimes can't trust other people. They don't know if they ever can and are scared to do so because of what their abuser did in the past.

Self-Doubt

Self-doubt stems from how you were treated by your gaslighters. The goal of those who gaslight is to make the other person feel worthless like their own thoughts and reality don't matter. Sometimes, those who have been gaslighted will hallucinate, and sometimes they'll see things that aren't there in order to make the gaslighted happy.

But the self-doubt extends past that. When someone how has been gaslighted all their lives finally leaves, they are often scared of what's next. They've been living with the reality of their abuser for so long that they don't know how to wrench themselves away.

This causes self-doubt. It's the doubt of oneself, the doubt of what's really out there, and the doubt of their own reality.

And boy is it terrible for you.

Self-doubt makes you second-guess everything that you do from here on out. After all, when you've been told you're worthless all your life, you probably will think that everything you do is worthless. But it isn't, that's just the gaslighted talking in your head.

Gaslighters love to do this because they know that, if you are continually taken down, if you ever do leave, you'll never really be yourself again, because you're scared to be. You'll be scared of expressing yourself, of being who you are, and you'll realize that, if you continue with this mindset, it will only make things worse from here on out, and for many, it can be a deadly action that can help erase who you really are.

This type of self-doubt can stifle creativity too and dreams as well, so remember that. You may feel like you should do something, but then, because you've been gaslighted in the past, you shy away from doing so. Oftentimes, this type of abuse will stunt your own creativity, and there is a reason why many people encourage those who have been gaslit to escape while they can.

Social Life Issues

Sometimes, gaslighting does affect your social life. The abuser will try their very hardest to keep the one who is gaslighted away from their friends, or even family too. The constant lying and saying they are bad people will happen. Lots of times, those who have suffered from gaslighting might end up never seeing their family until years down the road. This is something that can happen for a very long time.

What's scary as well, is that the person might end up completely isolating themselves from anyone, only relying on the abuser and nothing else. It can make the person feel like they're not capable of being loved, and also make the person feel like they're not stable, which is the scariest part about it.

For many people who have suffered the effects of gaslighting, they oftentimes will feel their confidence tank as well, since nobody seems to care about them or make an effort to go see them when in reality they're oftentimes being forced away from those relationships.

And what's scary, is that this can last a long time, even after you've left the relationship. Many who have been gaslighted in the past will not go back to their former friends and family right away, due to the effects of it. There is a reason why people will make sure that they seek out the help that they need, so they can reconnect with the person that they missed right away.

Difficulty Making Decision

Decision Making was done all from the abuser, and not very much from the person who was gaslighted. So, if you've experienced a bit of hesitation in decisions and have a history of abuse, you can probably thank gaslighting for that.

Decisions were left to the other person, and whenever you did make decisions, it was oftentimes seen as wrong, or incorrect to do. So why make decisions then?

That's why many, who have suffered from gaslighting in the past, can doubt the decisions that they make, from there, may not believe what they're doing is right.

This can lead to anxiety disorders in many cases. You're afraid of making decisions because whenever you did, you were always told that they were wrong. You were abused so much that you don't know what to do about anything anymore, so decision-making is very hard for those who've suffered from narcissistic abuse. Sometimes, this might seem like a couple of things are hard to decide, and other times, some people will just have trouble making any decision period.

Gaslighting can also make someone feel like their feelings and emotions don't matter, so they oftentimes have to choose what to do from a distanced viewpoint. So, instead of deciding from the heart, and in a way, that'll validate and help you, they're swimming in a pool of anxiety and stress, that isn't fun for anyone who suffers from this.

The Mental Health Side

There is also the mental health side of the effects of gaslighting. We did go over anxiety, but that's due to the confusion that the person makes the one who is being gaslit feel. The one who is being gaslit oftentimes doesn't know what's right and wrong, and they fear to do things. This can be a small occurrence, or this can be a major issue in their life that does need to be deliberated.

The one who is suffering from being gaslit may also feel a lot of hopelessness, along with self-esteem issues. This can also lead to depression, and oftentimes, people who are survivors of this oftentimes still feel like life is hopeless, that their feelings don't matter, and that they should never talk about it.

Depression is another major issue, since many times, being taken down so low for so long can make the person feel like it's not worth the energy as well.

PTSD is another one. After all, you were in a traumatic and abusive situation. The shock and stress from that person's actions still linger there, and it commonly develops from this.

Finally, codependency is something that can develop from this too. That's because you've been living a life where you had that type of relationship, and it can make you feel like you have to rely on others.

A Refusal To Show Emotions

This is a big one. This is due to the fact that survivors will always be on guard, always looking for the manipulation that's in any situation. Oftentimes, this can lead to people not trusting themselves, or trusting others either, and people do describe those who have suffered from this as always on guard.

They refuse to be vulnerable, for a good reason. They don't want to be hurt like that again. However, the problem with that, while it's a notable reason, it can be a problem for some people, since they'll refuse to show manipulation to the point where future relationships are stained, and they may have trouble holding a relationship because of this.

It does happen. Lots who suffer from this may even refuse to show emotions to others, staying single for a long time because they'd rather not be hurt, and would rather not experience what they did again.

CHAPTER 2
SIGNS YOU ARE MANIPULATED

The signs of gaslighting can be hard to see, especially for the person that is being manipulated by this tactic. Obviously, the effects of gaslighting are extremely detrimental. So, if you can recognize the signs of it as it is happening, it gives you an advantage and the possibility of getting out of this toxic situation before it completely destroys you and your life.

Oftentimes, people that care about you will recognize the signs before you will be able to. They may try and talk to you about the issues that they are seeing, but you may not be willing to hear them if the effects of gaslighting have already taken hold.

When someone you trust or once felt that you could trust comes to you and expresses their concern over signs of gaslighting, you should spend time reflecting on what they have to say to ensure that you are not a victim of this horrific abuse.

In this chapter, we are going to discuss a variety of different signs that you may witness if you are being gaslighted. Becoming a victim of gaslighting can impact your life negatively in every way. By looking over the following signs, it may become easier to understand what is going on, which can, in turn, give you the clarity and confidence to remove yourself from your current situation.

If you find yourself doubting your own emotions, you may be experiencing the repercussion of gaslighting. Oftentimes people will try to convince themselves that things really aren't so bad. They will assume they are simply too sensitive and that what they see as reality is tragically skewed from actual reality. If you have never had an issue with doubting your feelings, it can be a very good sign of gaslighting tactics.

Alongside doubting, your emotions will come doubting your perceptions of the events that unfold in front of you, as well as doubting your own personal judgment.

Many people that are being manipulated by gaslighting will be afraid to stand up for themselves and express their emotions. If you find that you are choosing silence over communication, it is a pretty good sign that gaslighting is present in your relationship.

These are normal feelings; however, if you are in a situation of gaslighting, you will feel this way consistently. You may always feel like you need to tiptoe around your partner, family member, or friend to ensure that they don't have a negative outburst. Additionally, you will start to believe that you are the one causing problems for them instead of the reverse.

The gaslighting narcissist will do their best to sever ties between you and the people that you care about. This can leave the victim feeling powerless and completely alone. The narcissist will convince their victim that the people around them don't actually care. In fact, they will try to convince the victim that everyone thinks that they are crazy, unstable, or flat-out insane. These kinds of comments make the victim feel trapped. It also causes them to distance themselves from the people that do actually care, which, intern, makes them in even less control than before.

Another sign that you are in the grips of the abuse that comes from a narcissistic gaslighter is feeling that you are crazy or stupid. The narcissist will use a variety of different words and phrases to make you question your own value. This can become extreme to the point that the victim may start repeating these derogatory comments. The sooner you can see the sign of verbal abuse, the sooner you will be able to make the decision not to let it deconstruct your sense of self-worth.

The gaslighting narcissist will do their best to change your perception of yourself. Let's say that you have always thought of yourself as a strong and assertive person, yet all of a sudden, you realize that your behaviors are passive and weak. This extreme change of behavior is a good sign that you are succumbing to gaslighting tactics. When you are grounded in who you really are and what your belief system stands for, it will be harder for the narcissistic gaslighter to get you to be disappointed in yourself. When you can recognize that the viewpoint of your worth has changed, it can give you the motivation to take back control of your own life.

Confusion is one of the narcissistic gaslighter's favorite tools. They will say one thing one day, and then the complete opposite the next day. The result of these types of actions is extreme confusion.

The behaviors of a narcissistic gaslighter will never be consistent. They will always try to keep you on your toes so that you are in a constant state of anxious confusion. This gives them more control. Finding that your partner, family member, or friend is exceptionally inconsistent with their behaviors should clue you into the fact that you are likely in a toxic relationship with them.

If your friend, partner, or family member teases you or puts you down in a hurtful way too, then minimalize the fact that your feelings are hurt. It is a surefire sign of gaslighting. Someone who truly cares about you, even if teasing, will take the time to acknowledge the fact that they hurt your feelings. If you are constantly being questioned about how sensitive you are, be aware you could be succumbing to the abuse of gaslighting.

Another sign that narcissistic gaslighting is occurring is when you constantly feel that something awful is about to happen. This sense of impending doom starts to manifest early on in gaslighting situations. Many people don't understand why they feel threatened whenever they are around a certain person, but after further investigation and getting away from the narcissist, they understand it completely.

Gut feelings should always be listened to, so if your body is telling you that something is not right between you and another person, you should remove yourself from the situation before things get terribly out of control.

There are constantly times in our lives that we owe other people apologies; however, when you are in a gaslighting situation, you will spend a plethora of time apologizing to people. You will feel the need to say I'm sorry regardless of if you have done anything wrong or not. You may really be apologizing for simply being there. When we question who we are and our value. It leads us to apologize profusely. If you notice how much you are saying, I'm sorry is increasing, and the things you are saying sorry for are minimal; you may be in a gaslighting situation.

Second-guessing yourself or constant feelings of inadequacy when you are with your narcissistic partner, family member, or friend are excellent signs that they are gaslighting you. If no matter what you do, it is never good enough, you should be aware that you may be being manipulated.

When it comes to 2nd guessing yourself, we're not just talking about second-guessing your decisions but second-guessing things like your memories.

You may wonder if you actually remember things as they happened because your narcissistic abuser constantly tells you differently. If you have never had a problem recreating and discussing your memories and all of a sudden you are trying to figure out whether or not what you are saying is true you may want to take a closer look at the person you are dealing with instead of looking at yourself.

Another sign that you are succumbing to the powers of gaslighting is functioning under the assumption that everyone you come into contact w/ is disappointed in you in one way or another. Constant feelings that you are messing things up are daunting and unrealistic; however, it is amazing how many people don't recognize when this is happening. They simply start to apologize all the time and assume that no matter what they do, they will make a mess of things, which will lead to others being disappointed in them.

When someone that you are in close contact with makes you feel as if there is something wrong with you, it could also be a sign of gaslighting. We aren't talking about physical ailments; we are talking about feeling as if you have fundamental issues. You may sit and contemplate your sanity and reality. Unless these were problems for you prior to entering into a new relationship, you should definitely pay attention to the sign.

Gaslighting can also make it extremely difficult for you to make decisions. Where you once made solid choices for yourself, you now have a sense of distrust in your judgment. This can make decision-making extremely difficult. Instead of making their own choices, many victims will allow their narcissistic abusers to make their decisions for them. The other alternative is not making any decisions at all. Obviously, this could have extremely negative impacts on a person's life.

One other great sign that you may be dealing with a gaslighting situation is when someone you are close to constantly reminds you of your flaws. Sure, a bit of constructive criticism is welcomed in most people's lives; however, when your weaknesses or shortcomings are constantly being pointed out by someone that is supposed to care about you, it's a clear sign that something is wrong. You should never despise who you are because of heinous comments made by a narcissist. So, if you take a step back & look at the people in your life, it will be easy to figure out who genuinely cares about you and who is trying to control you based on the way that they speak to you.

Along the same line, where a gaslighter will tear you down, they will almost never admit or recognize their own flaws. If their flaws are pointed out, it is likely that they will become aggressive.

The gaslighter is almost always on the offensive and ready to attack. This means that they will have an inability to recognize their own inadequacies and they will quickly place the blame on you if you try and point them out. They are excellent at playing the victim. Additionally, misdirection will be used so that they can turn things around and continue to dote on your shortcomings even if they are fictitious.

Another sign that you are being manipulated by a gaslighter is when you start to make excuses for their bad behavior. People will go to great measurements to cover up the abuse that they are facing and dealing with on a daily basis. They tell themselves and everyone else that things are OK or even better than OK. The victim will come up with a variety of excuses as to why their narcissistic counterpart is acting the way that they are. These excuses are not usually accepted by the people questioning the victim; however, the victim will just continue to make excuses rather than admit there is an actual problem.

CONCLUSION

There are people in the world who have been called "Gaslight" for doing nothing more than following the rules and being kind to those around them.

It is difficult to accept that in this day and age, a straight and level-headed person can be accused of being "Gaslighted".

However, it is clear that Gaslighting is alive and well in the 21st century. Gaslighting presents itself in various forms: false accusations of trauma, false accusations of sexual abuse, false accusations of cheating on taxes, fake emails requesting money from a new employer, false promises of a job promotion, false promises of a raise, false promises of a promotion at work, and many other forms.

We will examine the different types of Gaslighting (also known as gaslighters) and what to do when you come across one.

I've seen people get gaslighted for no reason at all. Some think they're just innocent victims who have been caught up in a game of psychological warfare. However, there are some people who are doing their gaslighting on purpose and with specific goals in mind. I decided to research this phenomenon and found quite a lot of information about the psychology behind the different types of Gaslighting. Here are some examples:

The Gaslighter's Goals, Motives, & Methods

They want to break down the victim's self-worth — causing them to question their own sanity. And if they break you, you will finally respond with anger instead of always taking it gently as you do now. This will make you sense ready for anything because you will be able to protect yourself now!

Gaslighting is an elaborate form of psychological manipulation. Gaslighting is a form of emotional abuse that involves systematic attempts to destabilize a victim's mental state. Commonly, gaslighting is used as a form of control, but it can also be used as a way to make someone doubt their own memories or perceptions.

According to Patrick Smith who wrote an article about gaslighting on Psychology Today, gaslighting is one of the most dangerous forms of abusive behavior. Smith suggests gaslighting can put victims in a situation where they are unsure of how to respond. If someone has their memories and perceptions undermined along with other aspects of their life, it can lead to serious psychological problems.

Fortunately, there are many ways people can protect themselves from gaslighting and other forms of psychological manipulation. First, people should have clear boundaries in their relationships when it comes to abuse. People should know who they can go to for help and should be familiar with any safety nets that are in place for them.

Understanding the definition of gaslighting can help people identify whether they are being subjected to this type of behavior in their relationship. Gaslighting needs to be taken seriously because it has been linked to serious problems such as anxiety, stress, and panic attacks as well as suicidal thoughts.

The advantages of Gaslighting

Gaslighting can be an effective tool because it causes its victims to question their own sanity. It is easy for the manipulator to convince the victim that they are losing their mind because the manipulator has perfected the art of confusing them. This allows the manipulator to gain more control in situations where they would not normally have any. Because their target is uncertain as to what is real or not, they will feel pressured into submission.

As stated earlier, the purpose of gaslighting can vary from person to person. It usually depends on what type of situation they are trying to enter into or maintain in order for them not to be in danger of being found out as a criminal or mentally unstable individual. Most often than not, people use gaslighting when they have friends or family members who could potentially expose them for doing something illegal or immoral. In these types of situations, a Gaslighter may try to convince their victims that there were actually a lot fewer occurrences than there actually were in order to cover up whatever type of crime that they had committed. In this scenario, Gaslighters will also use confusion and denial tactics such as repeating things back to victims repeatedly until they believe it themselves (as stated in "The conclusion of Gaslighting"). This way, if and when the victim does remember what was said and done, it will seem out of character for them and therefore will not seem dangerous in any way.